MINI ENCYCLOPEDIA *of*
GOLDFISH

A FIREFLY BOOK

Published by Firefly Books Ltd. 2015

Copyright © 2015 Interpet Publishing

First printing

Publisher Cataloging-in-Publication Data (U.S.)

Russell-Davies, Julia.
  Mini encyclopedia of goldfish : expert practical guidance on keeping goldfish plus detailed profiles of all the major varieties / Julia Russell-Davies.
[160] pages : color photographs ; cm.
Summary: "This encyclopedia will teach readers how to properly care for goldfish, which is more complicated than one might think" – Provided by publisher.
ISBN-13: 978-1-77085-610-3 (pbk.)
1. Goldfish. I. Title.
639.37484 dc23   SF458.C6R877 2015

Library and Archives Canada Cataloguing in Publication

Russell-Davies, Julia, author
      Mini encyclopedia of goldfish : expert practical guidance on keeping goldfish plus detailed profiles of all the major varieties / Julia Russell-Davies.
ISBN 978-1-77085-610-3 (paperback)
      1. Goldfish. 2. Goldfish—Varieties. I. Title.
SF458.G6R87 2015   639.3'7484   C2015-903973-8

Published in the United States by
Firefly Books (U.S.) Inc.
P.O. Box 1338, Ellicott Station
Buffalo, New York 14205

Published in Canada by
Firefly Books Ltd.
50 Staples Avenue, Unit 1
Richmond Hill, Ontario L4B 0A7

Printed in China   Originally published by Interpet Publishing

MINI ENCYCLOPEDIA *of*
GOLDFISH

Expert practical advice on keeping goldfish plus detailed profiles of all the major varieties

JULIA RUSSELL-DAVIES

Contents

Introduction

Oranda

Moor

Pearlscale

The goldfish is a member of the Cyprinidae variety of freshwater fish of the order Cypriniformes. All goldfish belong to a single species, *Carassius auratus,* and are members of the carp family (which also includes the Koi carp and the Crucian carp). The goldfish that we know today were first domesticated by the Chinese and have now been kept as pets for over a thousand years. After hundreds of years of selective breeding, goldfish now vary greatly in size, body shape, and fin configuration. They also come in a wide variety of colors, including white, yellow, orange, red, brown and black. This diversity is certainly part of their appeal to goldfish keepers. A tank of fancy goldfish can make an exotic and fascinating focus for any room, and owners can also become very fond of their pet fish. Goldfish can become tame and will learn to recognize their owners and to understand that humans are not a threat to them.

Today's goldfish have been bred selectively by Chinese, Japanese and European fish keepers for hundreds of years, and this has created some extraordinary goldfish varieties. Some of these are extremely weird and wonderful. "Fancy" goldfish varieties have very extreme characteristics, ranging from the slow-swimming black Moor goldfish, with their

◄ *Goldfish come in a fascinating variety of shapes and colors.*

Above: *Goldfish have been kept as pets for centuries and their popularity has spread around the world.*

Origins

The goldfish is a domesticated version of the carp, which was first domesticated by the Chinese.

CHINA

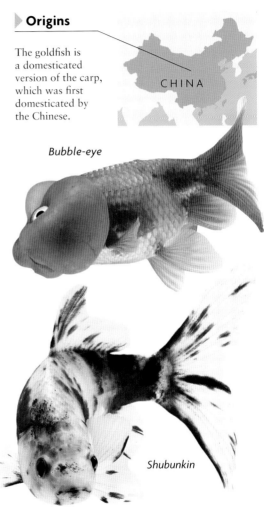

Bubble-eye

Shubunkin

trailing fins and boggling eyes, to the hooded and egg-shaped Ranchu (known to the Japanese as the "King of Goldfish"). It is extraordinary to think that all modern goldfish are derived from the plain but hardy wild brown carp. Early Chinese fish keepers of the Sung Dynasty period (960 to 1279 A.D.) were the first selective goldfish breeders. They noticed that the little brown river carp sometimes produced mutated golden fish with brighter, shinier scales and unusual fin shapes. It was during this time that individual fish, or pairs of fish, were first kept as pets in decorative shallow bowls, and the breeding of fancy goldfish began. These "mutated" fish were the forerunners of all of today's goldfish. The Common Goldfish, for example, is only one genetic step removed from the ancestral carp.

THE HISTORY OF THE GOLDFISH

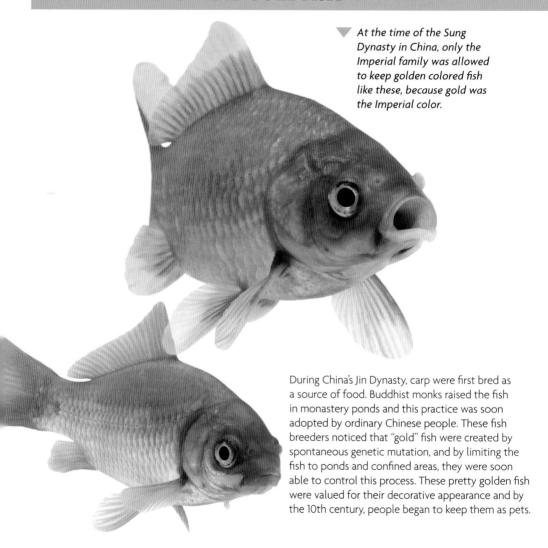

▼ *At the time of the Sung Dynasty in China, only the Imperial family was allowed to keep golden colored fish like these, because gold was the Imperial color.*

During China's Jin Dynasty, carp were first bred as a source of food. Buddhist monks raised the fish in monastery ponds and this practice was soon adopted by ordinary Chinese people. These fish breeders noticed that "gold" fish were created by spontaneous genetic mutation, and by limiting the fish to ponds and confined areas, they were soon able to control this process. These pretty golden fish were valued for their decorative appearance and by the 10th century, people began to keep them as pets.

By the time of the Sung Dynasty (960–1279), the Chinese Empress had ordered a special pond to be constructed in which to keep her red and yellow fish. Only the Imperial family was allowed to keep golden colored fish, as gold was the Imperial color. This was the reason that orange-colored fish became increasingly popular. White and red-and-white fish also developed. During the Ming Dynasty (1368-1644), goldfish were often kept in decorative bowls, either singly or in

Right: *The Chinese often displayed goldfish in decorative bowls in the house. They could be returned to a pond when the visitors had left.*

Bubble-eyes developed at the beginning of the 20th century.

The History of the Goldfish

pairs. Although these bowls were highly decorated on the outside, they were glazed plain white on the inside to show off the color and beauty of the goldfish themselves. This way of keeping goldfish made selective breeding much easier, and various mutations soon developed, such as double tail and anal fins, dorsal-less fish, short-bodied and egg-shaped fish. The first tortoiseshell goldfish were written about in the 13th century. These fish had snow white bodies and black spots.

By the 16th century, the goldfish had been introduced to Japan and this led to further selective breeding. This resulted in several new varieties, including the Veiltail, Ryukin and Tosakin forms.

Ryukin goldfish were developed by the Japanese in the 16th century.

▶ *Carl von Linnaeus*

Goldfish became particularly popular in Holland. In 1758, goldfish were first officially classified by the Swedish zoologist Carl von Linnaeus as *Cyprinus auratus*. Linnaeus (1707–1778) laid the foundations for the modern biological naming and the scheme of binomial nomenclature.

Red-eyed and globe-eyed goldfish, matt scales and calico fish were also developed. From Japan, goldfish were imported into Portugal from where they spread around Europe. They became highly sought after and their metallic-looking scales were considered to symbolize good luck and good fortune. Because of this, goldfish became a traditional gift for a first wedding anniversary. During the Qing Dynasty (1644–1911) bronze and blue goldfish were introduced.

As time went on, goldfish breeders continued to discover more and more fantastic forms, including multiple colored fish, different body shapes, fin styles and eye settings. Some of these forms of goldfish are extremely delicate and can only survive in specially constructed aquarium environments. Goldfish remain extremely popular in China, where around three hundred breeds are officially recognized. Breeding secrets are passed down from one generation to another. Goldfish have also found their way into Chinese art since the Ming Dynasty, in silks, ceramics and jade carvings.

The goldfish was first imported into the United States around 1850 and soon became a popular pet. The first American goldfish farm was established in Maryland in the late 19th century.

Oranda, Tigerhead, Pompom, Pearlscale, Shubunkin, Bubble-eye, Curled Operculum, Comet and Veiltail goldfish were introduced around the turn of the 20th century. The goldfish was also exported to Australia and New Zealand where it became equally sought after. The 20th century saw many more fancy varieties created by European goldfish breeders.

Above: *Goldfish remain popular in China and are often a subject for jade carvings.*

▶ *Oranda goldfish were introduced at the beginning of the 20th century.*

The goldfish is now a popular pet worldwide and this has led to many domesticated goldfish being released back into the wild. Although their conspicuous coloring means that very few of these fish survive for long, those that do often mate and breed with both wild carp and wild Koi carp. In particular, freed Shubunkin often survive long enough to mate with their wild relatives. The offspring of goldfish and wild carp pairings will be hybrids, but within three generations the majority of their descendants will revert to the olive/gray color of the wild fish. The offspring of goldfish and Koi carp matings are sterile.

GOLDFISH KEEPING TODAY

The goldfish is now one of the most popular pets around the world. There are many different reasons for this. Keeping goldfish is relatively inexpensive, after the initial costs of setting up an aquarium. The more popular varieties of goldfish are also cheap to buy, but even the simplest form of Common Goldfish is a graceful and attractive fish. They are relaxing and fascinating to watch and a perfect antidote to everyday stress. Goldfish are hardy and relatively simple to look after (although some fancy varieties are a little more demanding). Once the aquarium is correctly set up, goldfish are also relatively low-maintenance, and are often long-lived. An ordinary aquarium fish can live for up to 10 years, and some goldfish have been known to survive into their 40s. They also make responsive pets. While many people incorrectly believe that goldfish have a memory span of just a few seconds, they can actually remember events for at least

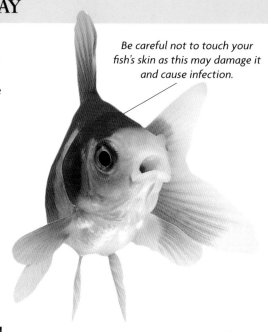

Be careful not to touch your fish's skin as this may damage it and cause infection.

Above: *The more popular goldfish are relatively cheap to buy.*

Above: *The goldfish are transported in an inflated bag to the new aquarium, preferably without delay.*

Above: *Common Goldfish are hardy enough to survive outside in a pond, but the fancy varieties need the constant temperature of an indoor aquarium.*

three months and recognize different people's faces as well as shapes, colors and sounds. They will definitely remember the person that usually feeds them, and will congregate where their food is normally sprinkled if they see that person anywhere near the tank. They can also be trained to take food from their owner's fingers (although you should be careful not to touch your fish's skin, as this can damage the layer of slime that protects it from infection). An aquarist will soon realize that each fish has its own personality, and some can even be taught to do tricks.

While the Common Goldfish is pretty hardy and can survive in outside ponds (if these have good water quality) where the temperature can fluctuate drastically, fancy fish usually need to be kept in

Above: *Goldfish will explore their tank environment and features like this bogwood make it more interesting for them.*

Goldfish Keeping Today

Each goldfish requires 10 gallons (45 l) of water to stay healthy.

an inside aquarium. Outside fish can survive in surprisingly low temperatures and will slow down their metabolism to survive in frozen-over water, almost as though they are hibernating. Indoor aquariums will need a good cleaning routine to keep the water clean and well oxygenated.

Happy, well-kept goldfish will play all day and explore their environment, so a large aquarium is a much kinder place to keep them. Goldfish also love company, and it is better to keep groups of fish, but each fish needs at least 10 gallons (45 l) of clean water to remain healthy. Goldfish will prefer mating in the breeding season, when their water gets warmer. They thrive when eating a healthy and varied diet (they are omnivores and will eat plants, insects, small crustaceans and even small fish). They can become bored and unhappy if they are fed the same food every day. Goldfish take naps when they are tired, although they don't have eyelids so their eyes stay open. As a goldfish's natural instinct is to flee from danger, their tank should be equipped with plants and caves in which they can hide. Goldfish are also naturally curious and will become bored and listless without toys or other fish to

Above: *Weigh down the roots of nitrate-absorbing weeds to stop goldfish from digging them up.*

Above: *Plastic weeds last forever and provide shelter and a spawning medium for goldfish.*

interact with. If they are put in a bare aquarium, depressed goldfish will settle to the bottom and only move when they are fed or frightened by sudden jolts. However, if you put your fish in a tank with gravel, aquarium accessories and plants (real or fake), they will make themselves at home and dart around all day. They particularly love to hide

behind plants or caves. They also need varied and tasty food to keep them happy.

Goldfish are not very territorial but you need to make absolutely sure that your fish always have enough room and water. Stress brought on by boredom or overcrowding is very bad for goldfish and can result in deviant behavior, including bullying and even cannibalism. Disease can also result from fish not having enough room.

When you add goldfish to a new tank you should not put in more than two at a time. This preserves the helpful bacteria in the tank which turn ammonia to nitrite and finally to nitrate. If fish are introduced in too great a number the bacteria balance can be adversely affected and the goldfish will die from breathing in an excessively high concentration of their own untreated excrement. Even if the tank has a good balance of bacteria, at least half of the water should be changed each week. Live aquatic plants will also help to improve the water quality as they take up nitrate.

Above: *Introduce just two new fish at a time to a tank to preserve the beneficial bacteria.*

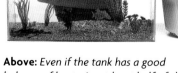

Above: *Even if the tank has a good balance of bacteria, at least half of the water should be changed each week.*

Clean plastic weeds regularly.

GOLDFISH BIOLOGY

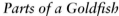

Reflective guanine produces the shimmering appearance of some goldfish scales such as this Ranchu.

To look after your goldfish well, it is very important to understand how their bodies work, and the functions of their various body parts.

What Gives a Goldfish its Color?

The goldfish has an outermost layer of skin called the epidermis. This forms a fine outer coating over the fish's scales. Its cells (the epithelial cells) are constantly shed and replaced by new ones. The epidermis also contains the slime cells that produce the mucoid secretions that form the protective slime coat. It is very important to preserve this protective coat, and you should make sure that your hands are always wet if you need to handle your fish. Beneath the epidermis, the fish's scales overlap to provide the fish with a flexible, protective armour coat. The scales themselves are transparent. Their color comes from the layer of skin and crystalline guanine that lies immediately

▶ Parts of a Goldfish

In order to care for your goldfish properly you need to know the name and position of its body parts.

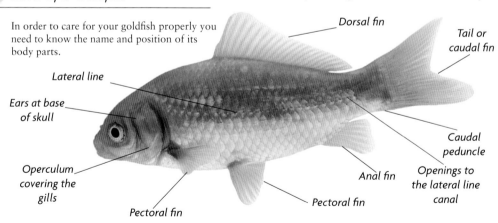

Dorsal fin

Tail or caudal fin

Lateral line

Ears at base of skull

Operculum covering the gills

Pectoral fin

Anal fin

Pectoral fin

Caudal peduncle

Openings to the lateral line canal

beneath them in the fish's skin. Guanine gives some fish a shimmering and glossy appearance (the Ranchu goldfish is good example of this). Fish with a matt appearance do not have guanine in their skin. The color of the fish depends on a number of different factors. The most important of these is the type and combination of the fish's pigment cells. Color is also environmentally influenced, light being the most important factor. Goldfish raised in a dim environment (such as deep ponds and rivers) retain a pale color, whereas fish raised in a bright environment develop brighter and more saturated colors. A fish's diet can also affect its color and a number of color-enhancing goldfish foods are available. A goldfish's color cells are shown in the image below.

White fish don't have any pigment cells. Fish change color from moment to moment as the melanin grains move within the pigment cells. When the melanin grains are dispersed they absorb more light and the fish darkens in color. When the melanin grains are arranged more closely, the fish looks lighter. The scales lie in the dermis, or the second layer of skin. This is made up of connective fibroblasts, collagen and blood vessels.

Goldfish that are kept outdoors and have greater exposure to natural light are usually more colorful than goldfish that are kept indoors.

Color and Scales

A goldfish's color cells can be categorized as follows:

Melanophores cells contain a brownish-black pigment called melanin.

Iridophores cells contain light-refracting and light-reflecting crystals that give a metallic sheen to a fish's skin.

Xanthophores cells contain yellow pigment.

Erythrophores cells contain red pigment.

How Do Goldfish Swim?

A fish's fins are crucial to its movement. They are made up of stiff rays covered by skin. The tail (caudal fin) and the muscular back part of the goldfish's body (the caudal peduncle) give the fish forward thrust by sweeping from side to side. Goldfish also have two pairs of pectoral and pelvic fins that act as steering mechanisms and brakes. They also help to prevent the head from pitching up and down. The dorsal fin on the fish's back acts as a keel to stop the fish rolling over as it moves forward, and the anal fins also help with this. When the fish turns in the water, all of its fins come into use. Fancy goldfish that have unusually-shaped fins may find swimming more difficult. These difficulties can become serious if fancy and Common Goldfish are mixed in a single tank. Common Goldfish, Comets and Shubunkins are much tougher and faster in the water than their fancy counterparts (including Oranda, Veiltail and Ryukin), and the latter may become stressed or injured when competing for food.

The dorsal fin functions like a keel to keep the fish upright as it swims.

All the fins are used when the fish turns in the water.

The front fins are used to steer the fish

The caudal fin moves from side to side to move the fish forward. This fish has a paired caudal fin, or tail.

The Swim Bladder

The goldfish's swim bladder is also fundamental to its ability to move in the water. This buoyancy aid is a gas-filled bag at the heart of the fish's body that enables it to hang motionless at the chosen depth. This is achieved by adding or withdrawing gas from the swim bladder.

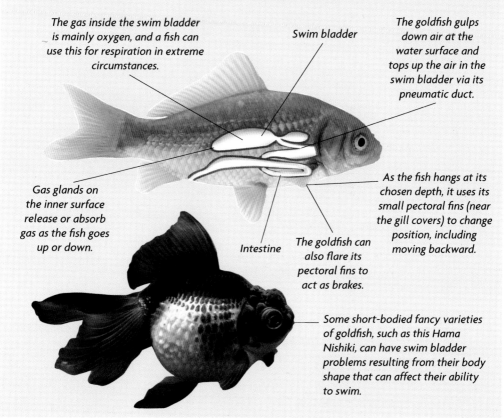

The gas inside the swim bladder is mainly oxygen, and a fish can use this for respiration in extreme circumstances.

Swim bladder

The goldfish gulps down air at the water surface and tops up the air in the swim bladder via its pneumatic duct.

Gas glands on the inner surface release or absorb gas as the fish goes up or down.

Intestine

The goldfish can also flare its pectoral fins to act as brakes.

As the fish hangs at its chosen depth, it uses its small pectoral fins (near the gill covers) to change position, including moving backward.

Some short-bodied fancy varieties of goldfish, such as this Hama Nishiki, can have swim bladder problems resulting from their body shape that can affect their ability to swim.

How Do Goldfish Breathe?

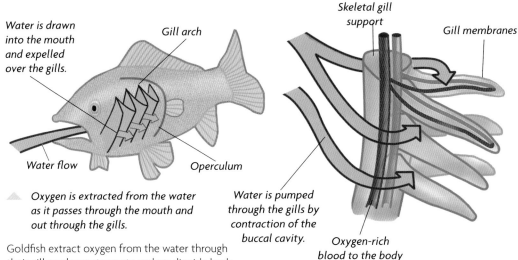

Water is drawn into the mouth and expelled over the gills.

Gill arch

Skeletal gill support

Gill membranes

Water flow

Operculum

Oxygen is extracted from the water as it passes through the mouth and out through the gills.

Water is pumped through the gills by contraction of the buccal cavity.

Oxygen-rich blood to the body

Goldfish extract oxygen from the water through their gills and excrete waste carbon dioxide back through the gills. The gills are covered by curved gill covers (operculum) and are perforated with five slit-like openings on both sides of the fish. These are arranged on a skeletal gill support. The opercula are clearly visible behind the fish's eye. The tissue between the slits is known as the gill arches. The fish has four gill arches on each side of its body. These are equipped with a delicate system of permeable blood vessels that are covered by a thin epithelium, through which the gases are exchanged. Water is drawn into the mouth and then pumped through the gills, where the gaseous exchange takes place. Oxygen then passes into the blood system of the fish, and carbon dioxide is extracted from the fish's blood. Well-oxygenated blood is crucial to the correct functioning of the fish's heart. This is

a simple four-chambered organ that pumps blood around the body through a network of veins and arteries delivering oxygen to the tissues. Clean, well-oxygenated water is crucial to this process.

The fish's gills are also crucial in the maintenance of its water balance. Salts and water are absorbed through the permeable membranes of the gills. The kidneys retain the fish's body salts but also remove excess water from the fish's body. The kidneys excrete ammonia through the gills as dilute urine. The gills also create a partial vacuum that helps the fish to suck up their food. Although goldfishes' mouths are toothless, they have teeth located well back in their throats that grind up the food as it goes down.

How Do Goldfish Feel?

Goldfish have six senses, one more than we do. They are acutely aware of the world around them and it is very important to a fish's well-being that all of its senses are properly respected and catered for. The goldfish uses its senses just as we do, to eat, reproduce, communicate and avoid danger.

Above: *Your goldfish rely on several senses to locate their food. When visibility is poor they will use smell, touch and taste to find it.*

The Sixth Sense

The nerve fibers in the goldfish's lateral line carries impulses to the brain and aid the fish in navigation.

The Lateral Line

If you closely examine a fish from the side, you will notice a line of special, slightly darker scales with tiny pores that runs from the fish's head to its tail. These pores are the openings to the fish's lateral line system (consisting of sensory cells and nerve fibers), which gives it its unique sixth sense. These nerve fibers carry impulses to the spinal cord and the brain itself. The lateral line system can detect minute electrical currents in the aquarium water and functions as a kind of echo locator so that the fish can identify its surroundings. It also enables the fish to locate other fish and avoid obstacles.

Lateral line

How Do Goldfish See?

Vision

Goldfish have simple eyes that can focus on objects that are both near and far. Many varieties of fish are nearsighted. Their irises can open and close, but more slowly than human irises. Their eyes can differentiate color, as well as ultra-violet and infra-red light. Their eyes are usually placed on either side of their head. This means than most fish have monocular vision, rather than the binocular vision that humans have. Because underwater visibility may be poor, goldfish do not rely on vision as a primary sense, but when the water is clear they can use their eyesight to locate food and other fish. They often have to use their senses of taste and

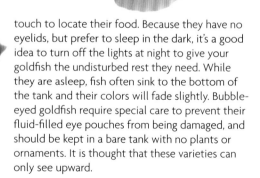

The fish has no eyelid and sleeps with open eyes.

Most fish have monocular vision with their eyes placed on either side of their heads.

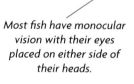

Bubble-eye goldfish need to be kept in a bare tank so that they do not damage their delicate eye sacs on toys or plastic weeds.

touch to locate their food. Because they have no eyelids, but prefer to sleep in the dark, it's a good idea to turn off the lights at night to give your goldfish the undisturbed rest they need. While they are asleep, fish often sink to the bottom of the tank and their colors will fade slightly. Bubble-eyed goldfish require special care to prevent their fluid-filled eye pouches from being damaged, and should be kept in a bare tank with no plants or ornaments. It is thought that these varieties can only see upward.

How Do Goldfish Smell?

Above: *Goldfish use their sense of smell when looking for a mate.*

Flaps guide the water in and out.

Water flows into the nostril as the fish is swimming.

Receptor cells respond to trace substances in the water and are interpreted by the brain as smell.

Goldfish nostrils are called nares.

Smell

By contrast to its vision, a fish's sense of smell is very highly developed. Goldfish have twin nostrils, which are called nares. Muscular contractions in the goldfish's nostrils help the water to flow through them into the olfactory pits. The nares are covered by flaps that guide the water in and out. Receptor cells in the nostrils respond to substances dissolved in the water. This generates nerve impulses that are relayed to the brain and interpreted as smell. The sense of smell is very important to goldfish as they use it to detect both prey and potential mates.

Taste and Touch

Taste

Fish have no tongues, but have taste buds on their lips and in their mouths as well as in the skin covering their heads, body fins, and barbells. Because of this, it is very likely that fish can taste their food before it goes into their mouths. They also use this highly developed sense to avoid any noxious substances in the water.

Taste buds on a goldfish's head may mean it can taste its food before eating it.

Take care when arranging the tank that the fish are not touched or stressed in any way.

Touch

Fish have a sense of touch but their tactile organs are not highly developed, apart from the lateral system. There has been a debate as to whether or not fish feel pain, but they certainly react to negative stimuli, so it is very likely that they do and should always be very gently handled with this in mind.

How Do Goldfish Hear?

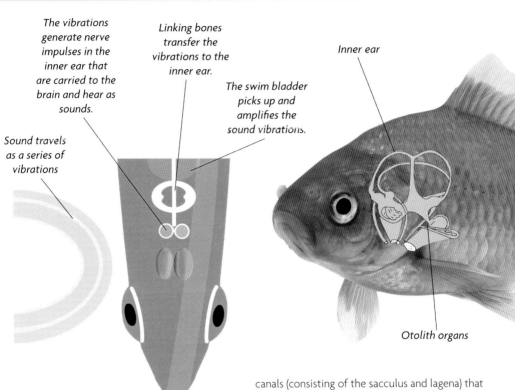

The vibrations generate nerve impulses in the inner ear that are carried to the brain and hear as sounds.

Linking bones transfer the vibrations to the inner ear.

Inner ear

The swim bladder picks up and amplifies the sound vibrations.

Sound travels as a series of vibrations

Otolith organs

Hearing

Water is an excellent conductor of sound, which is transmitted as a series of vibrations. Sound travels faster in water than in air. For this reason you should refrain from tapping your goldfish's tank as this can give your fish an unpleasant shock. Goldfish do not have external ears but have internal ear canals (consisting of the sacculus and lagena) that can translate the underwater vibrations. Linking bones (the otoliths) transfer these vibrations to the inner ear and these are then relayed to the brain where they are perceived as sound. The process also gives the fish its sense of balance. We know that fish make specific sounds during eating, mating and fighting, so being able to hear is essential to their survival and well-being.

Goldfish Varieties

There are now around 120 fancy goldfish varieties available to today's fish keeper. Almost every anatomical feature of the goldfish has all been changed by selective breeding and new forms continue to be introduced. The goldfish's eyes, body shape, finnage and coloration have all been altered by human intervention. Generally speaking, the more simple the form of goldfish, the easier they are to keep and the more suitable for the novice keeper. The Common Goldfish resembles

Above: *The Common Goldfish is preferred to more exotic goldfish by some because of its classic lines and more robust constitution.*

Above: *Generally speaking, the more simple the form of goldfish, the easier they are to keep and the more suitable for the novice keeper.*

its carp ancestors in every way except color and is also the hardiest of this species. Common Goldfish may be red, black, orange, white, yellow or bronze. Ironically, with its simple form and no exaggeration to distract the eye it is also one of the most attractive goldfish available.

Comet Goldfish also have a slim body and stiff fins. Unlike Common Goldfish, Comets have much longer fins and a deeply forked caudal fin that may be almost as long as the fish's body. Comets also come in a wide range of colors. They are hardy fish and can also survive in outside ponds. Comet and Common Goldfish can be kept together safely.

Left: *The Common Goldfish comes in a variety of colors such as red, orange, white and this rarer yellow, above.*

Above: *Slim-bodied goldfish can survive in very cool temperatures, including outside ponds.*

Above: *Fancy goldfish can be injured if they have to compete for food with Common Goldfish.*

Generally speaking, the more a variety departs from the ordinary goldfish shape, the more likely it is to need extra care. Because common or slim-bodied goldfish are tougher, more aggressive and faster swimmers than fancy goldfish varieties they should not be kept in the same living quarters. Fancy goldfish can become stressed or injured by Common Goldfish as they compete for food. Slim-bodied Goldfish are a good choice for an inexperienced goldfish owner. They are less fussy

Above: *Many children will enjoy a goldfish as a pet.*

Above: *A goldfish bowl is not usually a suitable place to keep your fish as it does not contain enough oxygenated water.*

about the water quality and can survive in very cool temperatures, including outside ponds. They can get quite large (over a foot long) in a large body of water. These larger fish will require at least 30 gallons (140 l) of clean water each. Although these fish are not hard to please, it is kinder to keep their environment as clean and pleasant as possible.

Keeping Common Goldfish is a wonderful way to start keeping aquarium fish. Many keepers then go on to keep more exotic and fancy goldfish as they become more experienced and confident fish keepers.

Goldfish Colors

The crown pearlscale has an egg-shaped body and thick domed scales which have a pearly sheen.

The Blue Oranda is a metallic-scaled fish and its blue coloration is most noticeable on its fins and the hood which covers its head.

Goldfish colors are now hugely variable, so that the term goldfish is now almost redundant. Matt black, blue, chocolate brown, orange-speckled, silver and scarlet goldfish are now available. Different scale types have also been produced by selective breeding, including domed and convex scales. Extreme coloration means that these fish wouldn't survive in the wild, but need to spend their lives in safe captivity. There are two further ornamental goldfish types, the metallic and the calico.

Metallic fish are the result of three gene types, metallic, bluebelly and mock metallic. They can be self-colored (red, orange, yellow, blue, brown and black) or variegated with silver. Metallic fish have reflective scales due to the layer of guanine under their scales. This makes their skin shimmer like metal. Some twintail or variegated metallic fish have only small areas of metallic color on their bodies; fully metallic fish are more highly prized.

Calico fish have a mixture of reflective and matt scales that are controlled by the presence or absence of guanine. They are recognizable by their beautiful calico pattern. They are derived from three gene types, calico, pseudo-matt and colored matt. Scales where guanine is present are called nacreous scales. Where the matt scales have no pigment under them,

Black goggle-eyed Moor

Shubunkins are prized
for their beautiful
calico patterns.

the fish skin appears pink. Pigment causes the fish skin to appear blue, violet, gray or brown. Only half of the descendants of calico fish are themselves calicos. Shubunkins are singletail calicos that have a balance of colors, reflective scales and a blue background. The more blue Shubunkins have, the more valuable they are considered is blue background Shubunkin means red brocade in Japanese. Shubunkins are recommended for novice goldfish owners and are recognizable by their beautiful calico pattern (pattern includes orange, yellow, red, brown, black, gray, white, purple, and blue colors). Like most slim-bodied

goldfish, Shubunkins are very hardy, competitive eaters, and fast swimmers.

The three most basic fancy goldfish body characteristics are egg-shaped, fancy fins and goggle eyes.

Egg-shaped Goldfish

Egg-shaped goldfish have compressed, short fat bodies. They include Fantails, Ranchus and Lionheads. A shorter swim bladder means that these fish are slower and less accomplished swimmers. This also makes them prone to diseases of the swim bladder. This can cause the fish to swim at a downward angle. Body compression can also effect the digestion of these fish and attention should be paid to their diet. Egg-shaped goldfish are very sensitive to poor water quality conditions and are only suitable for experienced fish keepers. They can't live in ponds as they are too delicate to survive in water that is colder than 60°F (16°C). Most egg-shaped goldfish shouldn't be kept with slim-bodied goldfish, as the egg-shaped goldfish may become victimized with fin nipping and may

Above: *This Ranchu has a classic egg-shaped body.*

be deprived of food. Egg-shaped goldfish need good water conditions, preferring at least 20 gallons (76 l) of aquarium water per fish, with 10 gallons (38 l) for each additional fish.

Right: *Egg-shaped goldfish should be kept in a tank that has no slim-bodied fish who might damage them.*

Fancy finned Goldfish

Left: *These graceful Veiltail Goldfish with their drooping fins are delightful to watch.*

Fantail

Fancy-finned goldfish have long, trailing, double fins. They are beautiful fish, calming to watch and can be a delight to own. Although fantails are one of the more basic fancy varieties, they have a simple, sturdy charm but they can be very challenging to successfully and consistently breed. Good fantails should have strong, stiffly held split tail fins with a deep fork and a good fan shape when they are viewed from above. The top lobe of the tail should not droop below the horizontal and the extremities of the fins should look even and rounded. Some fancy-finned enthusiasts prefer shorter fins while others prefer a slightly longer style of fins. The body should be deep and evenly rounded with no bumps, especially behind the head. As with all fancy goldfish, female fancy-finned goldfish tend to have deeper bodies. Breeding fantails can be challenging. Two fish with good color can often produce offspring with dull coloration and the same can be said for finnage.

Long fins can be quite vulnerable in a tank of mixed fish, and are prone to infections and parasites. Long-finned fish are slower swimmers and are also sensitive to water temperature.

The Oranda, Veiltail and Ryukin are all examples of fancy-finned fish.

Goggle-eyed Goldfish

Goggle-eyed fish have enlarged protruding eyes. This classification of fancy goldfish includes Globe-eye, Bubble-eye and Celestial goldfish. The Bubble-eyed goldfish is one of the most fragile and hard to care for variety of goldfish. These fish are a unique but entertaining type of coldwater fish. They look clumsy in the aquarium and lack a dorsal fin. With their blurred vision and poor sense of navigation, these fish are vulnerable to damage to their eye sac bubble, which can get punctured very easily. Bubble-eye goldfish are bred in different colors ranging from white, orange and red to calico and black. Celestial goldfish have upward-turned eyes. Young Bubble-eyed fish usually look quite normal as the bubble sac doesn't grow until the fish is around a year old. This first looks like an accumulation of fluid but as time goes by, the sac gets bigger and becomes more transparent.

All goggle-eyed goldfish need careful consideration as to how they are looked after. They need to be kept in large aquariums with calm water. Power filters, or under-gravel filter systems that generate strong currents in the aquarium water should be avoided. Any sharp objects that could damage the eye sacs should always be eliminated from their living quarters. Bubble-eyes should not be mixed with any other fish species as these may nip their eye sacs as they compete for food. Tiger Barbs, Swordtails and Guppies are particularly problematic. If your goggle-eyed goldfish do suffer some injury to their eye sacs, you can add a dose of a natural aquarium antibiotic, such a Melafix, to the water in your aquarium. These products are designed to fight mild bacterial infections, such as fin rot. Treatments should prevent secondary infection by other microorganisms. You should try to avoid adding any other chemicals or salt. The best solution is usually to leave the eye sac to heal by itself. But you should ensure that the aquarium water is perfectly clean

Globe-eyed goldfish

Below: *Bubble -eyed goldfish are only suitable for experienced fish keepers who can provide the care they require.*

and crystal clear to prevent any further infection. Healing can take up to two weeks.

Bubble-eyed fish are not usually sold in pet stores on the Internet. This is because the fish should not really be sold to inexperienced fish keepers. Because they need specialist care, a lack of this will inevitably result in a high mortality rate. They should not be added to general goldfish tanks. Bubble-eyed fish are usually sold only through specialist fish suppliers.

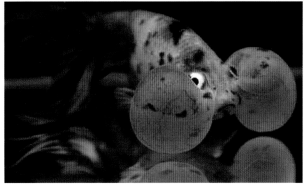

The Common Goldfish

Above: *The Common Goldfish is similar in shape to its wild ancestor, the Crucian Carp.*

The Common Goldfish (*Carassius auratus*) is closely related to the Crucian Carp (*Carassius carassius*) and can grow up to a length of 8–10 inches (20–25 cm) when it is mature and they need plenty of swimming space. The Common Goldfish has been instrumental in setting many hobbyists on the road to keeping more exotic fish and tropical species. Hardy and easy to keep, many children have had a pet goldfish of this type. The Common Goldfish (or hibuna) has no modifications from its carp ancestors apart from its color. Most fancy goldfish have been derived from this simple breed.

A good quality goldfish should have a similar body shape to its wild fish ancestors. It body depth should be no more than three-eighths of its body length, excluding the tail, and should have a gently curved dorsal profile. The fish's body length should be slightly more than twice its depth and should have a gently curved dorsal profile on which the fin should be erect. The caudal fin should be short and stumpy with short, slightly rounded lobes. The fish's other fins should be rounded. Goldfish have single caudal and anal fins and paired pelvic fins. Common Goldfish may be metallic and may be either self-colored or variegated. Some Common Goldfish colors include red, orange, yellow, blue, brown and black. Variegated fish may also include silver in their coloration. The pattern should be balanced and clear and extend into the fins. Common Goldfish are social animals that prefer to live in groups. They can interact with any fish belonging to the same species. With good care and plenty of attention, Common Goldfish can become really tame. They are quite visually aware and will soon be able to differentiate the face of their keeper and will swim toward them at feeding time. With

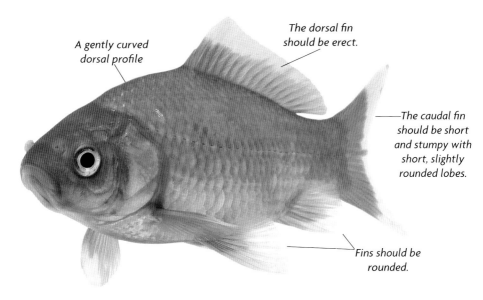

A gently curved dorsal profile

The dorsal fin should be erect.

The caudal fin should be short and stumpy with short, slightly rounded lobes.

Fins should be rounded.

The Common Goldfish

Above: *Common Goldfish are very sociable. When in a tank together, they may swim side by side with the other fish with their heads facing in the opposite direction.*

increased contact and familiarity, hand-feeding will soon become possible. Small goldfish will normally avoid human contact but middle-sized and mature goldfish seem to lose this fear. A full-grown goldfish is more likely to eat directly from the hands of its owner without any show of nervousness. Although goldfish owners enjoy this behavior, it can be dangerous to encourage this in outside ponds as predators can easily catch and eat friendly fish. Mature goldfish explore their environment through nibbling or grazing behavior.

Common Goldfish are very sociable. If they are moved to a new tank, they will normally try to communicate and familiarize themselves with its new friends by rubbing up against their bodies. They usually swim side by side with another goldfish with their heads facing forward. Alternatively they swim side by side with the other fish with their heads facing in the opposite direction or may even swim above other goldfish in a perpendicular fashion. Schooling is a common behavior when there is a new fish in the tank but this will soon cease so that each individual fish will swim and explore its surroundings by itself. Even if a new fish is introduced into a tank with a settled school of fish, aggressive behavior is uncommon.

An observant keeper may notice hierarchy among the fish during feeding time, which is quite common. This means that the larger goldfish usually get most of the food. However, small goldfish may also become aggressive or competitive feeders despite the presence of larger fish. This is a good indicator of the health of your fish as a willingness to feed shows that your goldfish are in good health.

Although Common Goldfish are often kept in relatively small bowls, this is undesirable as waste can soon build up to a toxic level, and the water can become de-oxygenated. Even a small goldfish needs at least 2–3 gallons (9–13 l) of clean water to keep it healthy. A good filter, with no heater, is recommended as these fish can grow to around 12 inches (30 cm) in length. Larger fish of this size may need up to 75 gallons (340 l) of water. If the fish don't get enough oxygen in warm weather, they may become unconscious or even die. But a water pump will expel carbon dioxide from the bottom of the tank and expel it. This will re-oxygenate the fish's environment as the bubbles break the surface of the water. A water pump should be able to cycle 10 times the volume of water in the tank per hour.

The hardy Common Goldfish can be kept outside in water gardens or outdoor ponds throughout the year, but it is still important to maintain good water quality. Natural and artificial pollutants both need to be controlled, including dead leaves, debris and algae. Outdoor ponds attract various plants animals and plants to become eco-systems of their own. If the pond temperature rises to dangerously high levels, this can kill the fish. In the winter, goldfish may become sluggish and stop feeding as their metabolism slows down. The pond must not be allowed to freeze solid and there should be an open spot in the surface ice to allow oxygenation of water. The ice should never be hit, as this sends shock waves of sound pressure through the water and will scare the fish.

Although Common Goldfish are hardy they can contract diseases if they are kept in bad conditions.

Above: *Some Common Goldfish colors include red, orange, yellow, blue, brown and black. Variegated fish may also include silver in their coloration.*

The Common Goldfish

Breeding Common Goldfish

Breeding Common Goldfish is relatively easy. A male goldfish in breeding condition will develop small white spots on his gill covers and a female goldfish will become plump. The male goldfish chases the female until she releases her eggs, then the male will release milt (seminal fluid) to fertilize them. The fertilized eggs stick to any available surface. You should remove the eggs to a separate aquarium before the adults eat them. When the fry hatch they can be fed with hatched brine, ready-made fry food or crumbled fish food.

Small white spots appearing on male gills show he is in breeding condition.

The male goldfish chases the female until she releases her eggs and he fertilizes them.

When these goldfish fry hatch, they should be fed with fry food.

Right: *The fertilized eggs stick to any surface and will be eaten by the fish unless you remove them to a separate tank.*

Right: *Goldfish have a natural lifespan of several decades.*

They produce quite a lot of waste and stir this into the water in their constant search for food. In small aquariums, illnesses can soon become fatal. Symptoms indicating sickness include cuts on the fins, a change in scale or eye coloration, excretions from the nostrils, scales falling off or fish frequently rising toward the water surface. Specialized treatments are available to manage specific diseases, but the first thing to do is to lower the temperature in your tank or pond to between 55°F and 60°F (12°C and 15°C). This will put the fish into semi-dormancy and slow down the progress of any disease. It will also reduce the effect of toxins such as ammonia.

Goldfish can live for years if they are fed a varied diet and housed in good water conditions. They have a natural lifespan of several decades and the longest lived goldfish on record lived to the age of 43. Poor quality care or life in a bowl greatly reduces a goldfish's lifespan.

Comet Goldfish

The Comet goldfish (or Comet-tailed goldfish) was first bred in the United States by Hugo Mulertt of Philadelphia in the late 1880s. The first examples were produced in the ponds of the United States Fish Commission in Washington. It is a single-tailed goldfish bred from the Common Goldfish and can be identified by its long, single and deeply forked tail. Comets' fins are longer and more elegant than the Common Goldfish. The caudal fin should be at least half, and ideally three-quarters of the length of the body. Its lobes should be pointed at the tips and held spread without folding or overlapping. Comets are also smaller and slimmer than Common Goldfish. An average Comet will be around 4 inches (10 cm) long, although they can grow to between 7 and 8 inches (18 and 20 cm) in a larger tank. If kept in a spacious pond, they can grow up to 12 inches (30 cm) in length in good water conditions. A

Comet needs at least 15 gallons (70 l) of water. Color-wise, Comets are primarily a reddish orange color but can also be yellow, orange, red, white and red-and-white. They may have red on the tailfin, dorsal fin and pelvic fin. They sometimes have nacreous (pearly) scales that give them a variegated color. Comets can change color naturally. These changes are thought to be due to diet and the amount of light a fish has been exposed to. Aquarists often report the reds and oranges of their goldfish changing to white. Giving your Comets a fresh diet, along with good lighting (with some shade) are suggested as the best way to maintain the original colors of your fish. Their tanks should be kept between 65°F and 72°F (18°C and 22°C).

Comets (*Carassius auratus auratus*) are very hardy and are another good fish for beginners to keep. They are inexpensive, readily available

Left: *The Comet's fins are longer than those of the Common Goldfish and it has a long, deeply forked tail.*

Sarasa Comets are red
and silver with long
flowing fins.

Above: *Comets come in colors other than orange
and are also known to change color.*

and most personable. They are very sociable and mild mannered and thrive in a community of fish. Comets do need plenty of swimming space as they are very active fish. They move around more quickly than other goldfish, and dart backward and forward around their tanks in a playful and fascinating way. Sometimes, they may even leap out of the water. This can be annoying to more sedate goldfish and may necessitate a lid on the tank for their own safety. Their elongated fins also give them an excellent turn of speed. The breed is also suitable for outdoor ponds and pools and may be kept alongside Koi. Although they are relatively easy to care for, they have a shorter life expectancy than Common Goldfish of around 7 to 14 years. They may live longer in optimum conditions. A popular variety of Comet is the Sarasa Comet.

These fish are red and silver and have long flowing fins. The fish are originally from China, although Sarasa is a Japanese word. The Tancho Single-tail Comet is another popular Comet-tailed fish. It is silver with a distinctive red patch on its head.

Bronze Comet

Shubunkin Goldfish

The Shubunkin is another very popular single-tailed goldfish. They are of Japanese origin and their name translates as "red brocade." Shubunkins are hardy, single-tailed fancy goldfish with nacreous scales and a pattern known as "calico." The variety was first created by Yoshigoro Akiyama around 1900 by crossing the Calico Telescope-eye Fish (Demekins) and the Common Goldfish. They have streamlined bodies with calico (multi-colored) markings. For show quality fish, at least 25 percent of the background color of the body must be blue. The best blue fish are produced from a breeding line of blue fish. Sometimes good blue fish may be obtained by breeding bronze (metallic) with pink (matt) goldfish, but a gray slate color may result. The fish should also be calico, with areas of violet, red, orange, yellow or brown with an even distribution of black speckles. The colors should extend right into the boundaries of the tail. They also have both matt and nacreous scales. These are a mixture of metallic and transparent scales with a pearly appearance. It may take several months for the nacreous coloration to develop on young fry. The term calico originally denoted three colored varieties of goldfish that did not include blue.

Shubunkins make excellent pond fish because they reach a length of 9–18 inches (23–45 cm) when they are fully grown at two to three years of age. In an aquarium, they usually grow to around 6 inches (15 cm) in length.

This popular goldfish is of Japanese origin and its name translates as "red brocade."

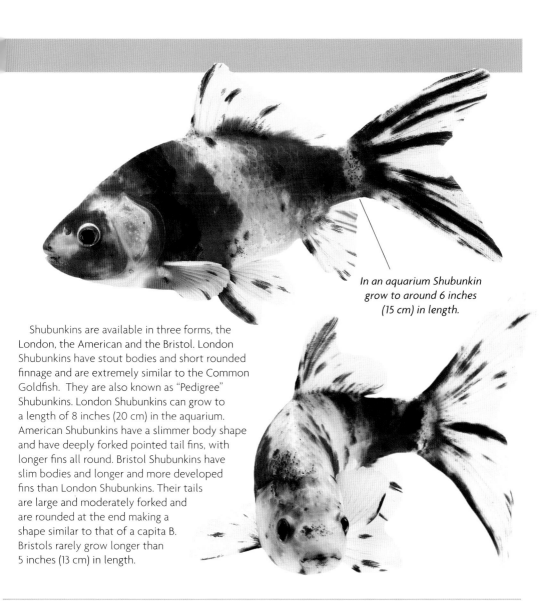

In an aquarium Shubunkin grow to around 6 inches (15 cm) in length.

Shubunkins are available in three forms, the London, the American and the Bristol. London Shubunkins have stout bodies and short rounded finnage and are extremely similar to the Common Goldfish. They are also known as "Pedigree" Shubunkins. London Shubunkins can grow to a length of 8 inches (20 cm) in the aquarium. American Shubunkins have a slimmer body shape and have deeply forked pointed tail fins, with longer fins all round. Bristol Shubunkins have slim bodies and longer and more developed fins than London Shubunkins. Their tails are large and moderately forked and are rounded at the end making a shape similar to that of a capita B. Bristols rarely grow longer than 5 inches (13 cm) in length.

Fantail Goldfish

Fantails are probably the hardiest variety of fancy goldfish and are a great option for the novice fish keeper. They can usually survive in the same conditions at Common and Comet goldfish and can be kept in both ponds or aquariums.

The Fantail goldfish is the western equivalent of the Ryukin. It has a rounded, egg-shaped body, no shoulder hump, a tall dorsal fin and a divided and forked double tail. The body should be at least three-fifths as deep as it is long. Apart from the dorsal fin, all of the Fantail's fins are in pairs. The fish also has double anal fins. The Fantail's fins are less developed than those of the Ryukin. The caudal fin should not drop or fold and should have a fan shape when viewed from above. The Fantail

goldfish type originated in the early 1400s during China's Ming Dynasty. These early fancy goldfish are the ancestors of most modern fancy goldfish. Fantails are a separate breed which has its own show standards. They come in a range of colors including red, orange, yellow and calico and can have metallic or nacreous scales. Ideally, the color pattern should be similar on both sides of the body. Young fish often have black pigment that may fade as the fish mature. The Fantail goldfish may have either metallic or nacreous scales. They may also have normal or telescope eyes. Telescope eyes do not develop until the fish is six months old. Although generally considered a hardy goldfish, the Fantail can be sensitive to prolonged exposure

Above: *Keeping Fantails in an aquarium requires an ideal temperature of around 73°F (23°C).*

Young fish often have black pigment which may fade with age.

Dorsal fin

Apart from the dorsal fin, all of the Fantail's fins are in pairs.

The tail should be fan-shaped when viewed from above.

to low water temperatures, which can cause swim bladder problems. Keeping Fantails in an aquarium requires an ideal temperature of around 73°F (23°C).

Fantails are slower swimmers than either Comets or Shubunkins but can live with other goldfish varieties. However, you should make sure that they are getting their fair share of food.

There are several Fantail varieties including the Metallic Variegated Fantail and the Metallic Sarasa Fantail.

Fantail Goldfish

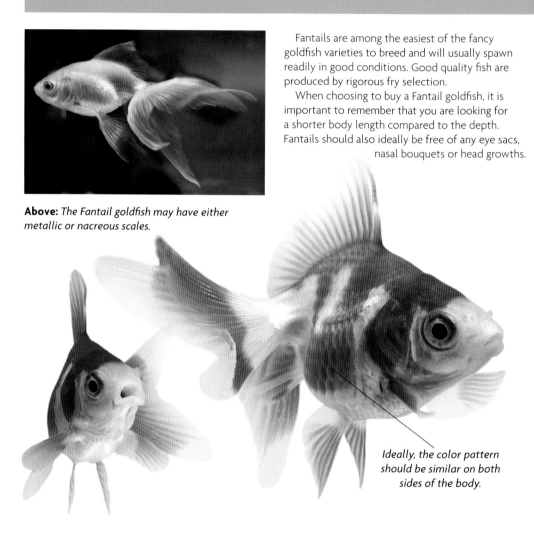

Fantails are among the easiest of the fancy goldfish varieties to breed and will usually spawn readily in good conditions. Good quality fish are produced by rigorous fry selection.

When choosing to buy a Fantail goldfish, it is important to remember that you are looking for a shorter body length compared to the depth. Fantails should also ideally be free of any eye sacs, nasal bouquets or head growths.

Above: *The Fantail goldfish may have either metallic or nacreous scales.*

Ideally, the color pattern should be similar on both sides of the body.

Feeding Your Fantail

Adults can be fed on daphnia, pellets and bloodworm while their fry should be fed on brine shrimp, daphnia and pellets.

Bloodworm

Daphnia

Brine shrimp

Fantails should be free of any head growths.

Fantails are prone to swim bladder problems if chilled.

Veiltail Goldfish

Above: *Veiltails have delicate, floating double fins.*

The Veiltail is one of the most lovely fancy goldfish varieties and is quite rare. They are a beautiful ornament to any aquarium, but need some specialist fish keeping to ensure their health and happiness. They are not recommended for beginners.

Veiltails were first developed in Philadelphia in the early 20th century. They were bred from the metallic Japanese Wakin fish, which was imported into the United States in 1893. Selective breeding created an elongated double-tailed goldfish variety and were originally known as the Philadelphia Veiltail Goldfish. In the Far East, the variety is called the Feather-dressed Long Finned Man-yu. Veiltails are similar to Fantails but have a more rounded body and long and delicate fins. Calico strains of the variety were produced by crossing them with calico Globe-Eyed goldfish.

Veiltails are quite delicate and it is quite difficult to breed good quality fish. Pairs often fail to produce offspring true to the parents and the fry are delicate. They have short, rounded and egg-shaped bodies with long and flowing tails. The body should be no shorter than 2⅛ inches (5.5 cm). This short body contrasts with the long and slender body of the Common Goldfish or Shubunkin. This has resulted in the variety having an extremely distorted swim bladder, which is prone to chilling. The breed's swimming ability is rather limited. Their bodies should be no more than two-thirds of the length of the fish and the dorsal fin should be long, around two-thirds of the depth of the body. It can sometimes be as long as 2¼ inches (6 cm) and it should be upright and not bend or sag. The pectoral and especially the pelvic fins should be long and narrow. Their long and delicate fins can be easily damaged, so their environment should be free from sharp rocks or other decorations. These injuries can lead to fungal and bacterial infections. The Veiltail's double caudal fins should be at least three-quarters of the body length and should not be forked or have pointed lobes. From above, the tail should appear to be divided. Veiltails can have any of the three types of goldfish scales and can be solid red or orange, variegated or calico in color. The colors should always be strong and extend to the fins.

Elongated goldfish varieties like the Common Goldfish, Comet and Shubunkin don't make good

Above: *A Veiltail's fins can be longer than its body.*

companion fish for the Veiltail. These much faster swimmers are too competitive during feeding time. Better tank mates for Veiltails would include the less hardy Celestial Eye, Water-Bubble Eye, Telescope and Lionhead goldfishes. If it is kept with other slow-moving varieties the Veiltail Goldfish should get plenty to eat and thrive. Veiltails should be bright and alert in appearance.

Ryukin

The Ryukin goldfish is a short, rounded and deep-bodied fancy goldfish with a characteristic hump its shoulder from which the back slopes steeply. Like many goldfish of this body shape, the Ryukin suffers from swim bladder problems. Their short bodies can also cause "dead zones" to form in their intestinal tracts where food can get caught. This results in constipation. Normally, when goldfish float upside down it is a symptom of swim bladder disorder. But with Ryukins, it can also indicate constipation. Overfeeding is the main cause of this condition, which can be cured by the fish being fed peeled green peas. These act as a laxative. Alternatively, you can stop feeding them for a day or two.

The Ryukin is a hardy and attractive fish with a pointed head and may be either long- or short-finned with a triple or quadruple tail. The dorsal fin is high and carried proudly. The caudal fin may be twice as long as the body with three or four lobes. Four lobes are the norm. A three-lobed tail should have a slight indentation. In Japan, this is known as the "cherry blossom petal tail." The Ryukin swims freely despite its large fins, which should be borne in pairs. It has normal eyes and no hood. Its head should be distinct from the body, with a "snout." The fish can grow up to 8 inches (20 cm) in length in good aquarium conditions. Ryukins come in several different color variations; deep-red, red-and-white, white, iron, chocolate and calico. Typically, they are metallic fish.

Although Ryukins look exotic, they are fairly easy to care for and suitable for beginners. They are quite hardy and, as they can tolerate temperatures only a few degrees above freezing, Ryukins can also be

Above: *The Ryukin can suffer from constipation and will be found upside-down if this happens. The cure for this is to feed a peeled green pea as a laxative.*

Below: *The Calico Ryukin has red, black, blue, white and orange markings. It can have either matt or metallic scales.*

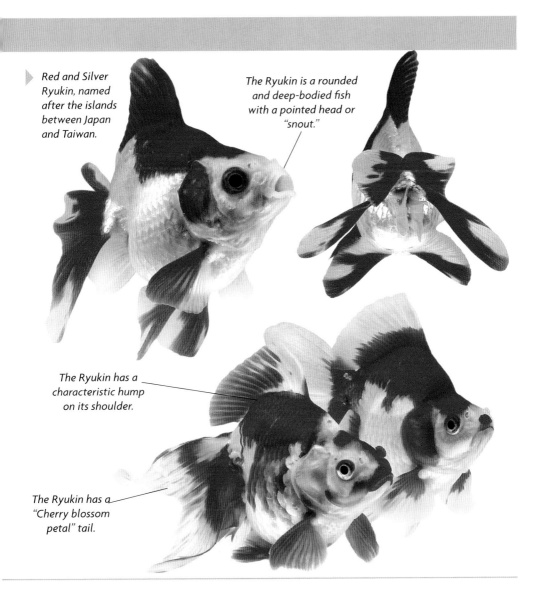

Red and Silver Ryukin, named after the islands between Japan and Taiwan.

The Ryukin is a rounded and deep-bodied fish with a pointed head or "snout."

The Ryukin has a characteristic hump on its shoulder.

The Ryukin has a "Cherry blossom petal" tail.

Ryukin

Calico Ryukin are every bit as colorful as Koi but require far less space to keep them in.

kept in outside ponds (although they are not quite as hardy as the Common Goldfish). The only downside to this is that the fish were bred to be seen from the side, so they look more elegant in an aquarium. Ryukins are every bit as intelligent as Koi, but require much less space. Even so, they should not be kept in tanks any shorter than 24 inches (60 cm) long. They also need more vertical space than many other goldfish and you should ensure that they have deep enough water to swim in comfortably.

The Ryukin is a vigorous feeder and will compete with weaker breeds such as the Celestial and Bubble-eyed goldfish. They may even become aggressive toward weaker breeds and should only be kept with fish with similar swimming abilities, such as Orandas and Lionheads.

The Ryukin comes from China, but it is reputed to have entered Japan via the Ryuku Islands (which are located between Taiwan and Japan). This is how the fish got its name. The breed is now very popular in Japan, where it is the Japanese version of the Fantail goldfish. The Ryukin was first referred to by name in a document of 1833. It was already known in Japan as the Onaga (longtail) or Nagasaki goldfish. In England, they were known as the Japanese Ribbontail, Fringetail or Veiltail.

The red-and-silver variety is the most prized by Japanese keepers. The best examples have a balanced pattern. The color should be a rich, deep red.

The Calico Ryukin has red, black, blue, white and orange markings. It can have either matt or metallic scales.

The Fringe- or Ribbon-tail Ryukin is a long-tailed version of this variety.

The Yamagata Kingyo (also known as the Sabao [mackerel tail] or Tamasaba) is a hardy single-tailed variety of the Ryukin. It was developed in Japan.

The Tetsu Onaga (or iron-colored longtail) Ryukin is a rare iron-gray colored variety of the variety.

Oranda Goldfish

Orandas were developed in Holland and have bodies that are deeper than they are long.

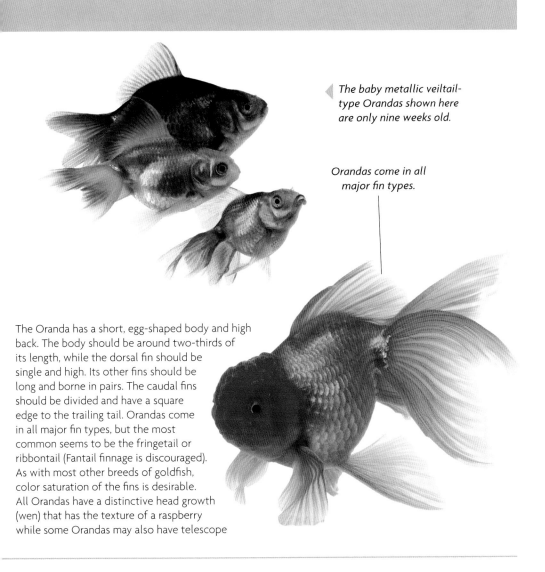

The baby metallic veiltail-type Orandas shown here are only nine weeks old.

Orandas come in all major fin types.

The Oranda has a short, egg-shaped body and high back. The body should be around two-thirds of its length, while the dorsal fin should be single and high. Its other fins should be long and borne in pairs. The caudal fins should be divided and have a square edge to the trailing tail. Orandas come in all major fin types, but the most common seems to be the fringetail or ribbontail (Fantail finnage is discouraged). As with most other breeds of goldfish, color saturation of the fins is desirable. All Orandas have a distinctive head growth (wen) that has the texture of a raspberry while some Orandas may also have telescope

Oranda Goldfish

A broad head is valued because it allows for a bigger hood or wen.

A red hood on a red fish shows the way the color differs when scales are not present.

eyes. The wen develops from white spots and a film covering on the top of the head, around the eyes and around the gills. The only exception to this is the Redcap Oranda, whose wen sits only on the top of their heads. Breeding standards for normal Orandas call for a full hood, but this should not be overdeveloped.

Orandas grow to around 8–10 inches (20–25 cm) in length, although fish of up to 15 inches (38 cm) have been known. Oranda are now the most well known of the exotic goldfish, especially in the United States and the Far East. The variety first appeared in the 1500s.

Orandas are not especially delicate, but they are not as hardy as Common Goldfish. They are not really suitable for ponds and should be kept in heated aquariums. They are vulnerable to diseases of the swim bladder and need to be fed a high quality, varied diet.

Oranda coloration is highly variable. Young fish may start out as black fish but this pigment is lost over time. Calico, blue, chocolate, red metallic fish and variegated are just some of the colors available. Calico Orandas are known as Azuma Nishiki in Japan.

There are several special varieties of Oranda. Tigerheads have a heavy wen growth on their faces and heads. They were first produced in the late 19th century.

Redcap Orandas have a red wen on the top of their heads. They should be completely silver apart from the blood red wen. Their fins should be pure white. They are very popular in the United States. Their beauty is in their simplicity.

Pompom Orandas (Hana Fusa fish) have red nasal bouquets on either side of their faces. These pompoms are formed from the nasal septum that

Redcap Orandas should be completely silver apart from the blood red wen on the top of their heads.

separates the two nostrils. Good quality fish have equal-sized pompoms.

Red Metallic Orandas have a red wen and a red body, but their body can appear orange under their layer of scales (as these reflect the light). Japanese fish keepers recognize many different shades of red in their fish.

Dragon Eye Orandas have telescope eyes.

Goosehead Orandas have a very tall head wen.

Celestial Goldfish

The Celestial Goldfish is also known as the Stargazer, Chotengan or Demeranchu. The most obvious feature of this small twin-tailed fancy goldfish is its protruding eyes that are located on the top of its head and stare upward, even when they are swimming forward. These eyes are known as telescoping eyes. Celestial goldfish were first bred in China in the late 18th century, although some keepers claim that they originated in Korea. The fish have no dorsal fin and their caudal fin should be similar to that of a Fringetail. It should be divided and be around half the length of the body or more, up to the full length of the body. It is not until the fish mature that their eyes telescope out and migrate around their heads. Because they are quite delicate, Celestial goldfish do not grow as large as other goldfish breeds and do not tend to live as long. They are one of the smaller breeds of Goldfish. Historically, Goldfish were kept in opaque ceramic bowls and only unusual specimens of the Celestial type could make eye contact with their owners.

A Celestial should have an elongated, egg-shaped body with a depth equal to a half to a third of the length of the body. A short body is preferred. The fish's back should be a smooth arch with no dorsal fin, humps or spikes. The Celestial's eyes should be level with each other and uniform in size and shape. They should point straight up from the surface of the head and be as large as possible.

Celestials are available in a wide range of colors. Most are orange or mottled orange and white, with the occasional white, red, black or Calico. As with other fancy goldfish, color saturation in the fins is favored. While they can have any scale type, metallic is most common. The ideal Celestial has dense, opaque color on its eye surface. The Celestial's eyes look normal at birth but soon start to migrate around the fish's head until they are pointing upward. This distinctive feature has been created by preserving a recessive gene.

From a keeper's point of view, Celestials are probably the most delicate breed of exotic goldfish. Celestials cannot see well and cannot compete for food with other goldfish, except the

Above: *Celestials do not grow as large as other varieties.*

The fish's back should be smooth and curved and its eyes should be matched in size.

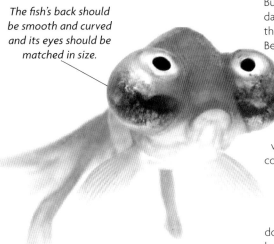

Bubble-eyed Goldfish. They are also vulnerable to damage from sharp objects. This is partly because these fish can't see what they are swimming toward. Because they can only see above, Celestials tend to sit at the bottom of the aquarium. If you keep Celestials, you should be careful not to have an overhead light fixed above your aquarium unless your fish have some cover that they can use. Celestials should be kept in warmer environments of 55°F (13°C) or higher. The variety can be kept in heated ponds that are kept completely free of any sharp objects.

There are several special varieties of the Celestial goldfish. Goggle Eyes are a Celestial variant. Their eyes are so upturned that they seem to face each other. Some Celestial variants do have dorsal fins and others also have nasal bouquets like the Pompom Oranda.

Bubble-eyed Goldfish

The Bubble-eyed Goldfish has a similar body shape and fin pattern to the Celestial Goldfish. They are the most exotic of the goldfish varieties. Like the Celestial, the Bubble-eye has the characteristic deep body, missing dorsal fin, and divided and forked caudal fin. All of their other fins are borne in pairs. The fish takes its name from the overdeveloped fluid-filled pouches (or bladders) under and around its eyes. The breed is relatively new, having been first introduced around 1900. It first appeared in China. The Bubble-eye originated as a mutant strain of the Celestial Goldfish.

Although the Bubble-eye's unique eye bladders are tougher than they look, they still need to be especially cared for. Any sharp objects should be rigorously excluded from your tank and your filter should be very carefully positioned so that the eye pouches can't get sucked into the intake. Any damage is likely to kill the fish as any rupture of the eye bladders is very likely to become infected. However, a damaged eye sac will sometimes heal itself. Like the Celestial, Bubble-eyes do not see well and this becomes more problematic as the fish matures and the sacs get bigger. Because of this, your Bubble-eyes should only be kept with other fish with which they can reasonably compete for food, such as the Celestial. Aggressive breeds, like the Ryukin should certainly be avoided. If you need to take your fish out of the water for any reason,

The Bubble-eye has a divided and forked caudal fin.

The main Bubble-eye body colors are orange, white, red, black, bronze and calico. This is a bronze.

The Bubble-eye doesn't have a dorsal fin.

The Bubble-eye's sacs grow larger with age.

Right: *Bubble-eyes often rest on the bottom of the tank.*

If you take your fish out of the tank for any reason, make sure the sacs are supported.

Bubble-eyed Goldfish

The eye bubbles tend to make these fish head-heavy.

Ideally the eye sacs are opaque and the same color as the fish's body.

The caudal fin should be about a third or half of the body length.

Above: *The slower swimming Bubble-eye would have trouble feeding in a tank with the swifter Common Goldfish or Ryukin. They are better kept alone or with other fancy varieties.*

the whole of the eye-bubble should be carefully supported.

An ideal Bubble-eye should have an egg-shaped body, with a depth of between a third and five-eighths of the body length. The fish should have no bumps or spikes along its back, but should form a smooth arch from its head to its tail. The dorsal contour should be quite understated, with no fin. The caudal fin should be about a third or half of the body length. The eye sacs should be uniform in size and as large as possible, but should not hinder the fish's swimming ability. Even so, the heavy pouches tend to wobble and make the fish's head heavy. Their eyes should turn upward, like the Celestial's. Bubble-eyes can grow to around 8 inches (20 cm) in length.

Although Bubble-eyes often have transparent eye sacs it is preferable for these to be opaque and the same color as the fish's body. The main Bubble-eye body colors are orange, white, red, black, bronze and calico. Bright yellow is quite rare. In pale Bubble-eyes, the blood vessels of the eye bubbles are clearly visible.

Bronze Bubble-eye Goldfish are bronze all over, even on their pigmented eye pouches. Their tails should be deeply forked and the dorsal fin completely absent.

Bubble-eyes lack a dorsal fin which contributes to their slower swimming speed.

Globe-eye Goldfish

The Globe-eye Goldfish is also known as the Telescope-eye, the Demekin and the Dragon-eye Fish. Black Globe-eyes are referred to as various kinds of Moor, including the Black Moor and the Panda Moor. These should be a uniform velvety black. Moor Globe-eyes can reach a length of 6–10 inches (15 to 25 cm).

The Globe-eye is an enduringly popular variety of goldfish. It is a fancy variety that is characterized by its enlarged and protruding eyes. These should be symmetrical, spherical and positioned at the tip of truncated cone-shaped protuberances on your fish's head. Its body shape is very similar to that of the Ryukin or the Veiltail. It has a deep body and long flowing fins, with a single, flowing dorsal fin. This should be erect when the fish is swimming. The other fins are paired, long and have pointed tips. The caudal fin should be long and forked to about three-quarters of its length. Globe-eyes come in a wide range of colors, including red, red-and-white, calico, black-and-white, chocolate, blue, lavender, chocolate-and-blue and black. Calicos should be bright with a blue background and brown, orange, red, yellow and violet patches, spotted with black. Globe-eyes may have either metallic or nacreous scales. A mature example of the variety should reach a length of around 4 inches (10 cm).

Because the Globe-eye has quite poor vision and delicate eyes, it should not be housed with more active goldfish or with any sharp objects. They have a tendency to swim into objects in the aquarium, so a larger tank is advisable (that holds at least 10 gallons (45 l) of water, or much more if you plan to keep more fish). As the fish is deep in shape, it needs deeper water to swim in, with a minimum tank depth of 20 inches (50 cm). They require a freshwater environment, clean water at the correct temperature 65°F–78°F (18°C–26°C) and pH value (6.5 to 7.5). They also prefer docile tank mates. Globe-eyes can survive for 10 to 15 years if they are carefully looked after.

A well-nourished Globe-eye will live longer. Because they can struggle to see small pieces of food, larger pellets that sink to the bottom of the

The protruding eyes are the defining characteristic of the Globe-eye.

The caudal fin should be long and forked to about three-quarters of its length.

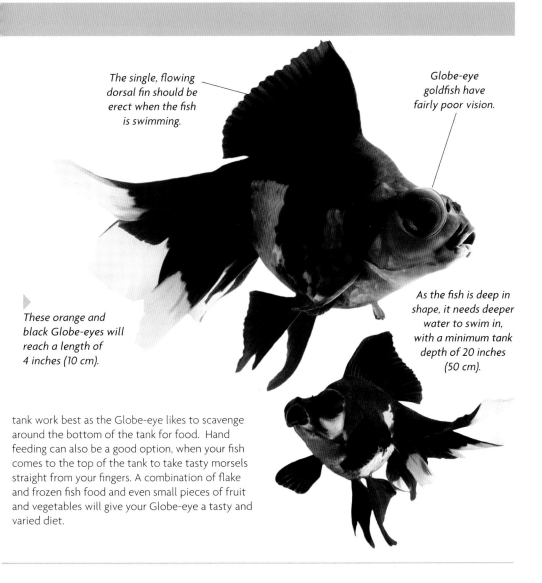

The single, flowing dorsal fin should be erect when the fish is swimming.

Globe-eye goldfish have fairly poor vision.

These orange and black Globe-eyes will reach a length of 4 inches (10 cm).

As the fish is deep in shape, it needs deeper water to swim in, with a minimum tank depth of 20 inches (50 cm).

tank work best as the Globe-eye likes to scavenge around the bottom of the tank for food. Hand feeding can also be a good option, when your fish comes to the top of the tank to take tasty morsels straight from your fingers. A combination of flake and frozen fish food and even small pieces of fruit and vegetables will give your Globe-eye a tasty and varied diet.

Panda Butterfly/Panda Moor Goldfish

Panda goldfish ideally have a deep black coloring on the eyes, back and fins with the rest a proper white rather than silver.

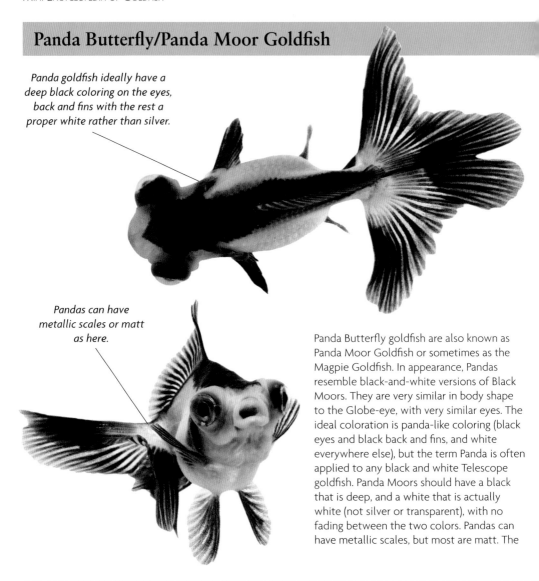

Pandas can have metallic scales or matt as here.

Panda Butterfly goldfish are also known as Panda Moor Goldfish or sometimes as the Magpie Goldfish. In appearance, Pandas resemble black-and-white versions of Black Moors. They are very similar in body shape to the Globe-eye, with very similar eyes. The ideal coloration is panda-like coloring (black eyes and black back and fins, and white everywhere else), but the term Panda is often applied to any black and white Telescope goldfish. Panda Moors should have a black that is deep, and a white that is actually white (not silver or transparent), with no fading between the two colors. Pandas can have metallic scales, but most are matt. The

It is important to remember that some goldfish go through color changes when they may look like Pandas, but only temporarily. Some unscrupulous pet store owners will try to pass these fish off as Panda Moors. Real Panda Moors retain their distinctive coloring into adulthood. Some Panda variants are orange (or another color) in place of white.

This relatively new variety of goldfish is becoming very popular and good specimens are both rare and sought after.

The Red Butterfly Moor is a variant of the Butterfly. As its name suggests, it is red and has the same butterfly-shaped tail at the Panda Butterfly. The fish has a touch of silver around its globe-shaped eyes and below its chin. The fish's tail is divided but not forked, in the style of a Veiltail.

Pandas can grow up to 6–10 inches (15–25 cm). Red Butterfly Moors achieve the same length.

fish is also noted for its long and beautiful caudal fin. From above, this resembles the wings of a swallowtail butterfly. Ideally, the caudal fin should be fully divided. The variety's eyes should be very similar to those of the Globe-eye.

The term Panda is applied to any black and white Globe-eye.

The Red Butterfly Moor

Ranchu Goldfish

No dorsal fin

Arched back

Downturned tail
and caudal fin

Hood

Fins are stiff and rounded.

The Ranchu is a hooded fancy goldfish, known as the "King of Goldfish" in Japan, where the variety was developed. It was originally bred from Chinese Lionhead goldfish and is now highly regarded by the Japanese. It is said that Ranchus are as highly regarded as Koi in Japan. The Ranchu has a strongly arched back (whereas a Lionhead's back is straight) and it also has a more downturned tail and caudal fin than the Lionhead. It does not have a dorsal fin and all of its other fins are borne in pairs. Its fins are stiff and rounded. Its wen or hood resembles a Lionhead Goldfish's, beginning at the bottom of the gill cover and moving upward. It should almost (but not quite) cover the eyes. This may take over a year to develop in young fish. The variety has an egg-shaped body with a deep belly. This is between

five-eighths and three-quarters of the length of the fish. This should be around 8–10 inches (15–20 cm) in a mature fish. Ranchus are hardy and very good swimmers.

Ranchus come in many colors, including orange, red, white, red-and-white, blue, black, black-and-white, black-and-red, natural, and chocolate. Their scales may be metallic, nacreous (calico) or matt. Ranchus with pale-yellow bodies and bright red heads are rare.

In Japan, Ranchus are popular competitors at goldfish shows, where they are judged with very precise standards. They are also one of the most expensive goldfish. There are several variants of Ranchu Goldfish.

The Red-and-Silver Metallic Ranchu is a traditional variety that has been bred for 250 years in Japan. They are intended as a top-view pond fish. This is a very popular Ranchu because the red head and wen and the silver body is such a great color contrast. This classic color combination is known as the Sarasa type. The bright red wen may take up to three years to develop. Fully grown, the wen covers the top of the head, spreads around the eyes and extends over the gill covers. These fish have a smooth dorsal profile. The Red-and-Silver Sarasa Ranchu's markings resemble those of the red-and-white Kohaku Koi. The Red-and-Silver Metallic Ranchu grows to between 8 and 10 inches (20 and 25 cm) in length.

Paired fins

▷ *Non-Sarasa Red-and-Silver Ranchus have red markings in an informal pattern on their body.*

Ranchu Goldfish

Non-Sarasa Red-and-Silver Ranchus have a fully developed red wen.

Red Metallic Ranchus are self-colored in a vivid orangey red.

Non-Sarasa Red-and-Silver Ranchus have red markings in an informal pattern on their body. They also have a fully developed red wen. They grow to the normal Ranchu size of 8–10 inches (20–25 cm) in length.

Red Metallic Ranchus are self-colored in a vivid orangey red. Despite breeders trying to achieve completely self-colored fish, most of these Ranchus have patches of silver. They have steeply angled backs and pronounced hood wens.

Jadehead Ranchus have white faces and white head wens. The rest of the fish is red-and-silver in a mottled pattern.

The Izumo Nankin Ranchu is also red-and-white but has almost no wen, and is predominantly snow-white with deep red variegated patterns. The color must be mostly white, and the head should have no

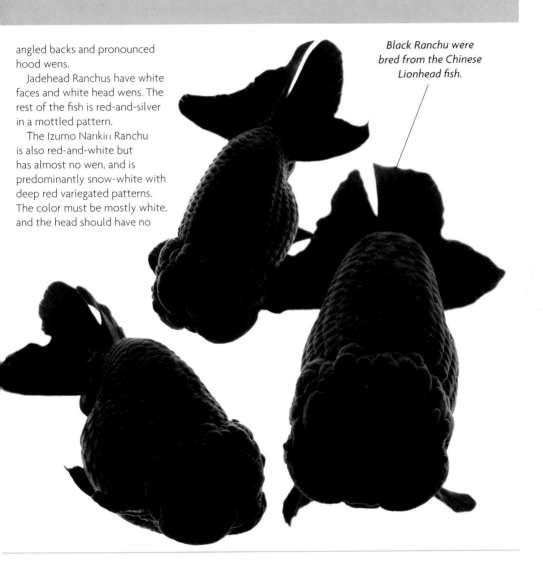

Black Ranchu were bred from the Chinese Lionhead fish.

Ranchu Goldfish

red coloration at all except for the lips or eyes. There are red markings on all fins and the tail. Nankins also have a pointed head. Their caudal fin is larger than that of an ordinary Ranchu, while their pectoral, pelvic and anal fins are smaller.

The Black Ranchu is very highly prized in Japan where they are considered as desirable as the Koi. The fish is a deep velvety black all over with no markings. They were bred from the Chinese Lionhead fish and resemble this variety. But they have a more steeply arched back and a fully divided caudal fin. They have a fully developed, even extreme, head wen that extends over the top of the head, around the eyes and almost covers the fish's eyes. Black Ranchus grow to around 8–10 inches

Above: *Calico Ranchu*

(20–25 cm) in length.

A multi-colored or mottled Ranchu is called an Edoni. They sometimes have complex variegated patterns.

The Edo Nishiki is a calico Ranchu. This variety was first produced in the 1950s by crossing a standard Ranchu with an Azuma Nishiki (calico Oranda).

Hironi goldfish are Ranchus which have been bred with Veiltail type fins. Otherwise they look like ordinary Ranchus.

Above: *Edo Nishiki*

These are juveniles and the wen is not fully developed yet.

Red and Silver Metallic Ranchus. These show the tail positioned perfectly and give an impression of restrained power.

Pompom Goldfish

Left: *The Pompom is a similar shape to the Bubble-eye but has dramatic nasal bouquets.*

The caudal fin should be forked and fully divided.

The Pompom, Pompon, Hana Fusa, *Carassius auratus* or Velvet Ball Goldfish is a type of fancy goldfish whose nasal septa have been bred with extraordinary bunches of fleshy lobes that form tight balls (or pompoms). These nasal bouquets occur on either side of the fish's head and can vary in size. They start to develop when the fish is around 18 weeks old. Sometimes, they hang down past the fish's mouth. They should not be so big that they are sucked into the mouth as the fish breathes. Good examples of the variety have a good color contrast between the pompoms and the rest of the fish's body (except in self-colored varieties where this should match the body color). An example of this would be the Chocolate Pompom where the bright red narial bouquet contrasts beautifully with the chocolate-and-silver body of the fish. In mottled and calico varieties, the pompoms

The pompoms are nasal growths that should be equal in size.

should match the body of the fish. They should be equal in size. The function of the fish's nostrils is to smell dissolved chemicals and odors in the water, and the pompoms should not inhibit this.

The Pompom's body shape and fins are similar to that of the Celestial or Bubble-eye Goldfish. The caudal fin should be forked and fully divided. The other fins should be borne in pairs and have a rounded appearance. Color saturation in the fins

is highly desirable. Some Pompoms have dorsal fins while others do not. Pompoms with no dorsal fish are classified as Lionhead types. Their backs should be a smooth arch from head to tail. The dorsal-finned variety (or Hana Fusa) is an elegant Japanese variant of the fish. It is also known as the White Pompom Oranda. Other Pompom varieties have Fantail-type fins.

Pompom Goldfish

Although they prefer a heated freshwater tank, Pompoms can tolerate coldwater tanks.

Nasal bouquets could be damaged by more aggressive breeds.

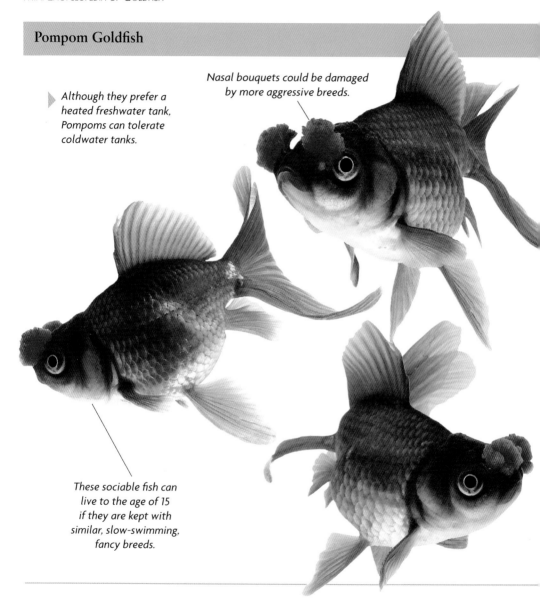

These sociable fish can live to the age of 15 if they are kept with similar, slow-swimming, fancy breeds.

The Pompom grows to around 6 inches (15 cm) in length. They should have an egg-shaped body, whose depth is at least half the length of the body. The variety has either metallic or nacreous scales and comes in a full range of goldfish colors including calico, chocolate, orange, yellow, black, silver, blue and red. Calico Pompoms should have a blue background with patches of color and black spots.

The Pompom's nasal lobes are quite delicate, but they don't interfere with the fish's vision. But the pompoms are prone to being nipped by aggressive varieties like the Ryukin, so the two varieties shouldn't be kept together as this will stress them. Pompoms are a slow-swimming and gentle breed. If the nasal bouquets are damaged, they may grow back but may not be completely symmetrical. Other more docile types (such as the Fantail, Ranchu, Black Moor and Oranda) make good tank mates as Pompoms are quite good at competing for food with similar types of fish. They prefer a heated freshwater tank but can also tolerate cold water.

All fins should be paired, and the caudal fin should be fully divided and forked. All fins should have a rounded appearance. There should be no dorsal fin in Pompoms matching the Chinese standard. As with other goldfish breeds, color saturation of the fins is desirable.

Pompoms have been heavily crossbred with many other types of goldfish, including the Celestial, Telescope, Oranda, Dragonhead and Lionhead. This has introduced the Pompom's distinctive nasal bouquets into many other varieties.

The Pompom used to be extremely popular, but has become less common in recent years. They are friendly and social fish and can live for between 10 and 15 years. Pompoms are omnivores and prefer a diet of pellets, flakes, live food, vegetables and fruit. This variety is recommended for the more experienced fish keeper.

All fins should have a rounded appearance.

Pearlscale Goldfish

The Pearlscale or Ping Pong Pearlscale Goldfish (also known as the Chinshurin in Japanese) is an unusually spherical-bodied fancy goldfish with highly unusual dome-shaped scales. Each of these is thickened at the center with a deposit of calcium carbonate that makes the scales appear like dimples on its golf ball-shaped body. The breed's fins are similar to those of the Fantail. They may be long or short and rounded at the edges. The dorsal fin is single; all of the other fins are carried in pairs. The caudal fin should be well divided, forked and held above the horizontal, with no signs of drooping. A Pearlscale can grow up to 6–8 inches (12–15 cm) in length, and should be no shorter than 2⅛ inches (5.5 cm). The depth of its body should be greater than two-thirds of its length. This short and rounded body can lead to disorders of the swim bladder that can make it difficult for the fish to swim and maintain a normal position in the water. This variety may have an Oranda-like growth (or hood)

The caudal fin should be well divided, forked and held above the horizontal.

Hood

Egg-shaped body

on their dainty heads, or have no head growth. They may also have two large bubble domes. The Pearlscale has a peaceful temperament.

Pearlscales come in a wide variety of colors including burnished metallic, self-colored, variegated, orange and calico. Calico fish should have a blue background color with patches of violet, red, yellow, orange, brown and spotted with black. Quality Pearlscales should have high color intensity with pigment extending into the fins.

Although Pearlscales are surprisingly hardy, their egg-shaped bodies can mean that their internal organs are overcrowded into their compact bodies. It is, therefore very important to avoid overfeeding. Pearlscales are very sensitive to cold water and should not be kept below a temperature of 55°F (13°C). They are also vulnerable to pH changes and should not be exposed to high acidity or alkalinity. The Pearlscale needs at least 30 gallons (136 l) of clean water for a healthy life.

The Hama Nishiki or Crown Pearlscale Goldfish

The Hama Nishiki (Japanese for Crown Pearlscale) was first bred by Shigeo Watanabe in Japan in 1975 and was first introduced to Japanese fish keepers in 1978. It has iridescent, pearl-like scales and an Oranda-like crown, hood, wen or head growth. This is a solid growth that appears above the fish's eyes, and is not filled with fluid. The Hama Nishiki is a cross between the Pearlscale and Oranda and may also be known as a Pearlscale Oranda. It has a rounded body and slightly longer fins than the Oranda but always has an Oranda-like head wen that develops as the fish ages. They may sometimes produce a pompom-like head growth. The fish's head itself should be pointed at the front. These fish are rounded, deep and broad. The Hama Nishiki has the same domed scales as the Pearlscale but usually has slightly longer fins than the Pearlscale or the Oranda. The breed comes in a variety of colors, including red, orange, black, and white and is usually found in a combination of these colors.

It may have either metallic or matt scales or a combination of these. The breed can grow up to 8 inches (20 cm) in length and is slightly longer than the Pearlscale. The Hama Nishiki is omnivorous.

Hama Nishiki/Crown Pearlscales need at least 30 gallons (136 l) of cold water and prefer a tank with a fine gravel floor stocked with hardy, coldwater plants. Crown Pearlscales love to dig, and may flick fine sand onto leaves which will damage less hardy aquarium plants. River rocks are more appropriate. Apart from its digging, the Hama Nishiki is a calm fish that swims around its tank sedately. If a Hama Nishiki loses any of its domed scales, these will grow back as normal flat scales, so this breed should be kept with similarly peaceable fish to prevent any unnecessary damage. Hama Nishiki are quite difficult to rear successfully, so are more appropriate for more experienced fish keepers.

Above: *The Hama Nishiki like to dig through the grit.*

The Hama Nishiki has domed scales.

Hama Nishiki can have either matt or metallic scales.

The breed originated in 1975.

Chinese Lionhead Goldfish

Above: *The Chinese lion dog whose head has a resemblance to the Lionhead goldfish*

Right: *The Lionhead is a delicate fish and so must not have anything sharp in its tank.*

Lionheads are one of the more delicate breeds of fancy goldfish and is not recommended for beginning keepers. They can't tolerate dirty or polluted water and at least a quarter or a third of their tank water should be changed once a week. They prefer slightly warmer water that should not be cooler than 60°F (16°C). The salinity should be kept low, at less than 10 percent.

The breed is named for the fleshy growth or hood that these fish carry on their heads, which resemble a lion's mane. The size of the hood varies between individual fish and it can sometimes cover the fish's eyes, mouths and nostrils. The wen is quite delicate and is prone to infection. If this is noticed, it should be treated immediately. The type was bred in China to resemble the mythical Chinese lion

dog, and is a descendant of the Eggfish (known as the Maruko in Japan). Its scientific name is the *Carassius auratus auratus*. These round-bodied fish grow up to 5 inches (13 cm) in length and need at least 10 gallons (45 l) of clean water in which to swim. Filtered water is best. The combination of the rounded body and the lack of a dorsal fin limit the breed's swimming ability. They have a peaceful disposition and are not suited as tank mates for the faster swimming and more competitive breeds like the Comet, Common Goldfish and the Shubunkin. Lionheads is an egg-shaped fancy gold fish and are the most popular of the dorsal-less goldfish breeds. They have double tail and anal fins. The breed is similar to the Japanese Ranchu in appearance, but can be differentiated by a flatter profile. The breed is similar in coloring to the Oranda and is available in the solid metallic colors of red, orange, chocolate, blue and black. Nacreous Lionheads can be calico, bi-colored

combinations of red and white (or red and black), or tri-colored combinations in red, white, and black. There is also a red-capped Lionhead, which has a bright red head and white body.

Lionheads are omnivorous and will eat all kinds of fresh, frozen and flaked foods. They like a balanced diet of flake food, brine shrimp, blood worms, daphnia and tubifex worms. Freeze-dried foods are generally safer and cleaner than fresh food. They need to be fed several times a day. Lionheads prefer a gravel-floored tank as they love to dig, this can damage live aquarium plants so silk plants may be preferable. Great care should be taken to avoid putting anything with a sharp edge in the tank, including plastic plants. Even smooth rocks or driftwood can injure the delicate wen.

Lionhead goldfish lay eggs and will spawn if they are kept well in good conditions. They are moderately easy to breed.

BUYING YOUR FIRST GOLDFISH

Before you buy your goldfish, you should set up an environment that will be appropriate for your new fish. This will mean that you will need to decide what goldfish varieties you plan to buy in advance. Most beginners start with a few Common Goldfish. While these fish are not particularly difficult to look after, they will need a good-sized aquarium, a filtration system, heated water, lighting and tank decorations. This needs to be set up in advance and the water has been properly "cycled" so that it

Above: *If any of the fish in the store have any signs of illness, do not buy fish from the store.*

will have the right level of good bacteria. This will ensure that it will be a happy and healthy home for your new pets.

The first decision you will need to make is where you want to buy your fish. The most important thing is to source healthy, disease-free fish that will be a joy to keep. This means that you should give careful consideration to where you source your new pets. The quality of fish you are able to buy can vary massively depending on whether they have been kept in suitable conditions. Taking advice from more established goldfish keepers is a good idea, but you could also go around and check out some of your local pet stores. May areas have a choice of independent pet stores and/or breeders and pet store chains. Inevitably, some of these stores are better than others. But there are several signs that will help you to identify a good and caring fish supplier, which should have all of the following:

- **Large, uncrowded fish tanks** that enable the fish to swim freely in clean water.

- **Tanks with efficient filter systems** to keep the water crystal clear.

- **Clean-looking tanks** with clear glass and algae-free water. They should smell pleasant.

- **No dead fish in the tanks**. Apart from being a bad sign of how the fish are being kept, it shows that the store is not paying their fish enough attention.

- **Healthy looking fish**. If any of the fish in the store appear ill or have injuries, white spots or any other signs of illness, do not buy fish from this store. Tinted water may indicate that the fish are being treated for some kind of illness or infection. This isn't a good sign.

- **Knowledgeable staff.** You should be able to ask the store staff for advice, and they should appear interested in the welfare of the fish.

- **A calm and peaceful environment**
Loud music stresses fish and makes them more prone to illness.

- **Free water testing.** A good pet store should be happy to test the water in the aquarium you have set up to ensure that it is suitable for the fish you plan to buy. Indeed, a responsible pet store should not sell you any fish until your water quality is good enough to support them.

Generally speaking, you should only buy a few fish to start with. It is best to buy small, lively fish that are swimming briskly around the tank and showing interest in their surroundings. You should avoid any fish that are gulping air at the water surface or have any wounds, split fins, damaged scales or red or white spots. Any marks on the fishes' bodies could indicate a bacterial infection. The fish should have a good body shape with no wasting or hollows, erect fins and a clear color. You should pay particular attention to the fishes' stomach areas, where problems can often begin. Don't be tempted to buy a weaker-looking fish that you feel sorry for; it will only cause heartache later.

Don't get carried away and buy too many fish for the aquarium you have set up. You should allow a

Above: *A good pet store should have staff to advise you when you are choosing your fish.*

minimum of 24 square inches (150 sq. cm) of water surface area for each 1 inch (2.5 cm) of fish length. So a tank that measures 24x12x12 inches (60x30x30 cm), with a surface area of 288 square inches (1,800 sq. cm) can accommodate about 12 inches (30 cm) of fish. You should make sure you know this measurement before visiting the pet store. Of course, you also need to factor in that your fish will grow, so you should know the adult length of any fish you buy. For reference, an aquarium of this size has a water capacity of 12 gallons (55 l).

Buying Your First Goldfish

Once you have chosen your fish, the dealer should gently isolate them in the tank with a soft net and then scoop the chosen fish in their hand to transfer them into a large plastic bag. The bag should be inflated and carefully sealed so that there is plenty of well-oxygenated air in the bag with the water. The bag corners should be carefully taped over so that the fish can't get caught in the corners and hurt themselves.

You should take your fish home as soon as possible, to reduce the stress of being kept in a smaller volume of water. It may help your fish to remain calm if the clear plastic bag is covered with an opaque bag. A paper bag or a black bin liner is ideal. This should be carefully supported in an upright position. You should not let your fish get either too hot or too cold on their way home. An insulated box is good to protect the fish from heat, with scrunched up paper to keep the bag upright.

Right: *Transport your fish carefully in a plastic bag with oxygenated air inside it.*

In winter, a cloth-lined shoebox will insulate the fish against the cold. Your fish are very aware of any movement, so they should be carried very carefully and driven with care.

Once you get your fish home, you should try to give them the best possible start. To do this, you need to acclimatize them to their new home as gently as possible. Float their plastic bag in your tank before releasing the fish. This is to enable the fish to get used to the temperature of the water in the tank (which should be 62°F to 68°F (17°C to 20°C). Dumping your new fish into water that is either much warmer or cooler than the water in the bag may shock them, so spending quarter of an hour equalizing the temperature of the water in the bag to that in the aquarium is much kinder. Your tank water should have been given at least a couple of weeks to allow any chlorine to dissipate, give beneficial bacteria time to grow allow the pH level of the water to balance. Once the temperature of the water in the bag and the water in the tank has equalized, open the bag very carefully. Let the stale air dissipate. You should then add around half a cup of aquarium water to the bag. Let this sit for a couple of minutes, then add another cup of aquarium water and wait for a couple more minutes. Continue this process until the bag is filled with aquarium water you can then very gently lift the fish with a net and release him into the tank. This will prevent any dirt or bacteria contained in the store water being released into your aquarium. You should dispose of the water in the bag and the plastic bag straight away.

Left: *A paper bag will protect the fish from stress on their way to your tank.*

Above: *Float the bag on the tank until the water temperature is the same.*

Another important factor in your fishes' environment is the level of light. Bright light is stressful to fish. As most pet stores are dimly lit, your fish should be protected from the bright light outside on your way home. You should also keep the lighting rather subdued in the room where the tank is placed, and avoid direct light from a light fitting or a window. Leave the room and aquarium lights off for a few hours after your fish have been released into their tank. Your fish have undergone a significant lifestyle change and need to become relaxed and calm in their new environment. Once the fish are safely in the tank, you can replace the aquarium condensation tray. Overfeeding is very ill-advised at this early stage. Any uneaten food will clog the tank filter, so it would be better to wait for a few hours until the fish have acclimatized themselves to the tank and are starting to feel hungry.

Above: *Add aquarium water to the open bag a cup at a time. Gently release the fish.*

Buying Your First Goldfish

Newly homed fish may sometimes look a little pale; this is brought on by the stress of moving to their new home. They may also feel a little shy, and hide among the plants and rocks in the aquarium. They will soon come out when they feel a little more confident. It you are unlucky enough to lose a fish at this early stage of stocking your aquarium, don't panic, but try to find out why this has happened.

Once your first fish have settled in, you can add more, gradually. You should wait at least a couple of weeks before you add any new fish. You should also do a water test for ammonia and nitrite to assess the water quality in your aquarium before adding more fish. If you can detect either of these substances you should not add any more fish until these substances have gone. You should also check your existing fish over to make sure that they look healthy and unblemished. Goldfish are sociable creatures and naturally prefer to live in shoals of at least six fish.

Above: *Let your first fish settle into their new tank for a few weeks before you introduce any new ones and remember that the sociable goldfish likes to have a shoal of at least half a dozen.*

Setting Up Your Aquarium

Install a dimmer switch.

This is a good location for your aquarium, which will need an electric socket nearby but not directly underneath.

Direct sunlight may cause algae.

Avoid radiators.

Doors in constant use can stress fish and drafts can upset temperature of tank.

Only use shelves if they are purpose-built to hold the weight.

Avoid placing the tank near loudspeakers or a TV as the vibrations will distress fish.

The process of setting up your aquarium is very important. It will ensure that your fish will enjoy their lives and that you will be able to enjoy them. There are several important decisions to make that will decide how healthy and successful your aquarium will be. The most important factor in any tank will always be the quality of the water, but there are several other safety considerations that you should observe.

- You should place your aquarium away from areas with fluctuating temperatures (drafts or heat), direct light (including sunlight) and cooking fumes. Too many people passing by can also cause drafts.

- A room with many windows, like a sunroom, is unsuitable. The light will be too bright and the day and nighttime temperature will fluctuate wildly.

- Vibrations from a frequently opened/closed door are undesirable.

- Your aquarium needs to be near an electrical supply.

- You should not spray anything near the water of your aquarium including furniture polish, air freshener, hair spray or deodorant.

- You should replace the aquarium hood to prevent anything falling in to the aquarium, or other animals trying to scoop out the fish.

- You should always wash your hands after touching the aquarium water.

- If you reduce the volume of water in the tank, turn off the water heater.

Bowl or Aquarium?

Above: *This modern goldfish bowl incorporates an air pump and a filtration system.*

Above: *This aquarium comes with a cabinet to support the weight of the water.*

Although modern goldfish bowls provide much more humane and pleasant environments than the oxygen-depleted, narrow-necked, unfiltered goldfish bowls of the past, they are still not as fish-friendly as aquariums.

Modern bowls have much larger water capacity and can be equipped with electric filter pumps to maintain water quality. A largish bowl can hold around 7 gallons (30 l) of water.

Fancy goldfish generally prefer an aquarium, and it is better to invest in the largest that you can afford and accommodate. Goldfish thrive when they have space. A purpose-built stand or cabinet

is also a good investment. Placing your aquarium at ground level can be dangerous. Young children may bang on the glass and crack it, or put foreign objects into the water. It might also be a trip hazard. A stand raises the fish to a good viewing height where you can observe them and check on their health and well-being more easily. Most stands have adjustable screw feet on each leg that can be used to level the tank. Modern aquariums often also have custom-built hoods with integral light fittings and a condensation tray to protect these from being splashed by the water.

Coldwater Aquariums

Most new fish keepers begin with a coldwater aquarium; these are suitable to keep common goldfish and some of the fancy goldfish varieties that are the result of selective breeding. The goldfish's wild cousins live near the bottom of slow-moving rivers, and creating a natural looking and interesting environment for your pet fish can be one of the most exciting parts of keeping goldfish.

You should also remember that you will always need to maintain a clean and salubrious environment for your fish. Goldfish and other coldwater fish eat ravenously, and excrete copiously, so you will need a good quality and well-maintained filtration system to cope with this waste. An oversize filter might make sense, but you will also need to maintain a rigorous cleaning and maintenance schedule.

Despite the effort involved, a coldwater aquarium can be a delight. Another factor you need to consider is that, in centrally heated homes, the coldwater aquarium is rarely truly cold. Normal room temperature is perfectly acceptable for most aquarium coldwater fish and aquatic plants. But to avoid stressful variations in temperature, your tank should be fitted with a combined heater/thermostat. This should be set around 70°F (21°C).

Below: *A mixture of plastic and real plants will create a colorful environment for your fish.*

Aquarium Sizes and Capacities

Tanks and aquariums are sold in several standard sizes. As you can see, even a moderately large tank will contain a considerable weight of water and you need to be sure that your floor will support this, especially if the tank is positioned upstairs. You may want to double check this with a structural engineer.

Height/Width/Depth	Water Volume	Water Weight
24 x 12 x 12 inches (60 x 30 x 30 cm)	12 gallons/55 liters	120 pounds/55 kg
24 x 12 x 15 inches (60 x 30 x 38 cm)	15 gallons/68 liters	150 pounds/68 kg
36 x 12 x 12 inches (90 x 30 x 30 cm)	18 gallons/82 liters	180 pounds/82 kg
36 x 12 x 15 inches (90 x 30 x 38 cm)	23 gallons/104 liters	230 pounds/104 kg
48 x 12 x 12 inches (120 x 30 x 30 cm)	24 gallons/109 liters	240 pounds/109 kg
48 x 12 x 15 inches (120 x 30 x 38 cm)	30 gallons/136 liters	300 pounds/136 kg

Glass or Plastic?

The most commonly available aquarium is still the rectangular glass tank with which we are all familiar. Other shapes including corner units are also available. Vertical designs are also obtainable but these have a relatively small water surface area and require a powerful pump to circulate the water to ensure that it is sufficiently oxygenated.

sizes and may be more expensive than the glass equivalent. Acrylic is also less refractive than glass and can easily be drilled or molded into many different shapes. On the downside, acrylic tanks need to be supported across the top to prevent them from bowing apart under pressure from the weight of the water.

Modern aquariums are available in either glass or acrylic. Both have their advantages. Glass is strong, rigid, clear, easy to clean and scratch resistant but is four to ten times heavier than the equivalent amount of acrylic. Glass can also shatter if subjected to a sharp blow. Tempered glass is stronger but cannot be drilled to accommodate your tank equipment. Glass also refracts light and can make your fish appear distorted.

Acrylic tanks are virtually indestructible but scratch very easily and can become cloudy and yellowish. They are usually only available in smaller

Vacation Tanks

If you plan to keep only a couple of fish, you may decide to buy a vacation tank so that you can take your fish to a friend or relative's house while you are on vacation. Because of the smaller volume of water in these tanks, you must make sure that they are really well filtered.

First Steps

When you bring your aquarium home, you should position it carefully and make sure that it's level. It's a good idea to use a spirit level to double check this. If your level doesn't span the tank, use a piece of board that you can rest the spirit level on. The next thing to do is to give the aquarium glass a

Left: *Clean the inside of the aquarium glass with plain water and a clean cloth.*

Below: *Use a glass cleaner only on the exterior of the tank to avoid introducing chemicals into the water.*

Above: *Use a spirit level to check that your tank is level.*

Left: *The feet of the stand can be adjusted.*

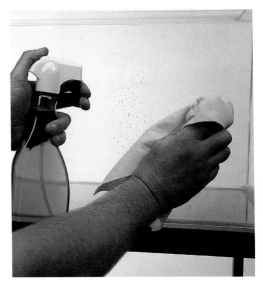

good clean, both inside and out. Any fine dust that has collected on your tank will leave an unpleasant film on the water when you fill it. Inside the tank, just use plain water to clean the glass, and a clean cloth. It's safe to use glass cleaner on the outside glass, but you don't want to add any chemicals to the aquarium water itself.

Substrate

The next job is to add your chosen substrate. This is the gravel that lines the bottom of almost all fish tanks. Although aquarium gravel is sold as having been washed, you should rinse this very thoroughly in several changes of clean water. This gets rid of any dust in the gravel. You should use about 3 inches (7.5 cm) of gravel as this is sufficient to root a selection of aquarium plants.

Choosing the right substrate for your aquarium is an important decision. The most important consideration is what would be good for the health of your fish, and whether or not you want to grow plants in the substrate medium. Your choice will also have an impact on the aesthetic appeal of your tank.

There are four main considerations when you choose your substrate medium: the size of the particles, their color, how they will react to the water and how they will affect your fish.

Above: *Place gravel into the tank using a jug rather than dropping it from a height.*

First Steps

Note: There are some situations where you may not wish to use a substrate, for example in breeding tanks, quarantine tanks, and nursery tanks. It is easier to catch fish in a tank without substrate. On the negative side, no substrate means that there is nothing to hide waste or uneaten food and this may be unsuitable for fish that need to dig. Fish may also become spooked by their own reflection in the glass of a bare-bottomed tank.

River sand

Fine gravel

Coarse gravel

Medium gravel

Polished pebbles

Black gravel

Colored gravel

Particle Size

The particle size of substrates varies greatly from the finest sand to river rocks. Both have advantages and disadvantages. Fine substrates can compact and lead to a depletion of oxygen in the tank and may even start to release hydrogen sulfide. This is extremely toxic to fish. Fine substrates can also be difficult to clean. On the positive side, river sand won't damage bottom-living fish. Large particle substrates, such as polished pebbles, can trap uneaten food and lead to a toxic build up of rotting matter.

Setting Up the Aquarium

Choose colored gravel that is nontoxic.

Some fish like to move substrate around. Over-fine particles can irritate fish but larger ones may be unsuitable for fish that like to make nests in the substrate. You will need to research the specific needs of your fish.

You should also consider the smoothness of the substrate. Glass chips with sharp edges may hurt your fish and may not be suitable.

Particle Color

Choosing the color of your substrate is more than just an esthetic decision. Fish don't like substrates that are too pale. They reflect the overhead light and make spook the fish and make them feel insecure. Pale substrates can also make fish look too pale, but dark-colored fish can look great against pale material. Pale substrates also tend to make your aquarium look larger, but they will show any fish waste more clearly. Dark substrates, such as black gravel, tend to show off the colors of the fish better, making light-colored fish look brilliant. But dark substrates can also make your tank look smaller. On the positive side, a brownish-colored substrate will hide fish waste quite effectively. While some people prefer the substrate to look as natural as possible, others like something more eye-catching.

Particle pH

Substrate can also be used to affect the pH value of the water in the tank, either to raise or lower it. Crushed coral for example will raise the acidity of the water while peat moss will lower it. The safest thing is to look for an inert substrate that won't affect the pH value of your tank water.

Above: *A gravel that is natural in color appeals to some, while others favor something that complements their fish.*

Setting Up the Aquarium

Gravel

Gravel is the most popular substrate used by goldfish keepers and is ideal for creating a natural appearance in your tank. You can slope the gravel slightly from front to back. Around 3 inches (7.5 cm) is a good depth. Gravel comes in many different grades (fine, medium and coarse) and a range of colors. Most aquarists prefer smaller grade gravel that won't allow food debris to settle through it and make it difficult to keep the tank clean. But this can pack down if it's not cleaned regularly. Medium-sized gravel is suitable for most aquarium sizes and filter systems, but it can lodge in a small fish's throat. Coarse gravel is best for larger tanks. It can be mixed with medium gravel for a stream-bed effect. Larger gravel can also get stuck in a fish's throat. You should always buy lime-free gravel and look for any white shell debris that might make the water too alkaline. It is also important to avoid sharp-edged gravel, especially if your fish are diggers.

Gravel comes in lots of different colors. Black gravel shows off the color of the fish really well.

You can also buy artificially colored gravel, but you should double check that this is nontoxic. White gravel is unpopular with most fish. It reflects overhead lights and makes the fish feel insecure.

Once you have washed your aquarium gravel you can transfer it to the tank by hand or with a jug or container.

Polished Pebbles

Polished pebbles look highly decorative in your aquarium, but droppings and uneaten food can lodge between the stones.

Polished pebbles

Below: *This yellow Comet shows up well against the red gravel.*

Setting Up the Aquarium

Sand

Sand is another good substrate medium that won't damage bottom-living fish or compact down. It is available in a huge range of different colors from pale to black. It is widely available and inexpensive. It does have downsides, however. Because it is so fine, it is difficult to clean your tank without removing some of the sand, although food debris will settle on the top of the sand rather than filtering through it. Dirt will also show up on pale-colored sand. If you do decide to use sand as your substrate, you will need to make sure that you use a filter that can cope with it and won't get blocked too easily.

Sand can also become easily compacted and stagnant. Aquarium plants can find it difficult to root in this medium.

Above: *Fluorite is available pre-washed but should still be rinsed thoroughly.*

Crushed Coral

Crushed coral can raise the pH value in the aquarium and is not a good choice for most goldfish. It is also light in color, which most fish dislike. It is also poor at hiding dirt and debris and needs frequent vacuuming to keep it clean.

EcoComplete

EcoComplete is a natural-looking and long-lasting substrate medium that is ideal for aquarium plants. It contains all the mineral nutrients that plants require to thrive.

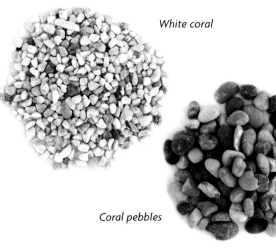

White coral

Coral pebbles

Fluorite

Fluorite is a clay-based substrate with very high iron content. It is stable, porous clay gravel that gives a natural-looking aquarium. It can also be mixed with other gravels and will last for the life of the aquarium. Fluorite is available

Above: *Africana aquasoil keeps the water clear.*

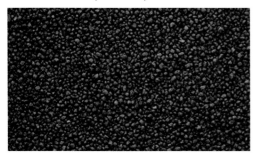

Above: *Amazonia aquasoil is one of three varieties available.*

in various brand names. It is not chemically treated and will not change the pH of the water. The medium is not recommended for plants that have delicate roots. Although the substance is pre-washed, it still needs to be rinsed thoroughly to remove any residual dust. The water may become cloudy at this stage but this should clear in a few hours.

Laterite

Laterite makes an ideal lower layer of substrate for planted aquariums. It is subtropical clay that contains high levels of iron oxide. The medium retains nutrients for your aquarium plants that they can use through their root system. It is usually baked to make sure that it is sterile. Like Fluorite, Laterite may cloud the tank water for a while.

Aquasoil

Aquasoil is a natural aquarium substrate. It is available in three different varieties and is made of small round grains. The material acts as a passive filter. Africana is red-brown in color and is produced in hard granules that keep the water clear. Malaya is ocher in color and long-lasting. Amazonia is dark black-brown in color.

Potting Soil

Potting soil is cheap and natural, and is a good growing medium for aquarium plants. Negatively, soil or compost can compact and/or clog your filter. It is also difficult to know if commercial composts have any toxic additives.

Laterite

Setting Up the Aquarium

Above: *This amusing novelty wreck should not be used for fish with delicate trailing fins.*

Above: *This deep sea diver should be checked for any sharp edges.*

Aquarium Décor

For many fish keepers, one of the most exciting things about their new hobby is decorating their aquarium. There are so many lovely tank decorations available that one of the most difficult things is to decide on a theme! You may prefer a natural look, a novelty theme or an underwater fantasy. Whatever you choose will impact on your fish, so you need to make absolutely sure that the décor you decide on will be completely suitable and safe for your goldfish. They will enjoy having places to shelter and different areas in which to play.

Most aquarium decorations fall into two main categories, fake and organic. "Live" rocks are particularly suitable for the freshwater goldfish aquarium as they are teeming with beneficial bacteria and microorganisms that will help to clean the water. But as with all the aquarium ornaments you decide to put into your tank, you need to be absolutely sure that they don't have any sharp edges that could hurt your fish.

Other organic tank decorations might include bamboo canes, well-washed glass bottles, real aquarium plants, bogwood and natural driftwood. Mopani wood is also popular for its interesting and varied colors. Sand-blasted Mopani wood is pale and heavy.

Fake, or manufactured decorations might include replica plants (silk or plastic) artificial rocks (ceramic or plastic), fake wood (ceramic or plastic) and lots of different novelty items in various different materials (such as castles, divers, sunken galleons, cartoon fish and treasure chests).

Air-operated ornaments can be particularly useful, as they agitate the water surface and provide some welcome movement in the tank. An air-operated diver is a popular tank addition.

Aquarium suppliers offer a wide range of both natural and artificial rocks. The smooth contours of water worn rocks look the most natural and have no sharp edges to injure your fish. Natural rocks include slate (rock and pebbles), limestone, pebbles, boulders, volcanic lava, granite, hard coal and sandstone. Artificial rocks include grotto ceramic, rainbow rock, ocean rock and manufactured colored rock. Grotto ceramic is particularly useful as it is both inert while supporting bacteria in its porous surface. Grouping larger rocks towards to the back of your tank, and odd-numbered groups

Above: *Weathered glass bottles are an attractive addition to the tank.*

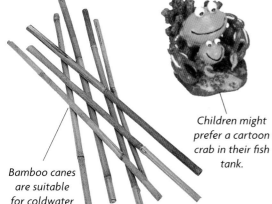

Children might prefer a cartoon crab in their fish tank.

Bamboo canes are suitable for coldwater tanks.

Above: *Hard coal can be used with black gravel and should be scrubbed first to remove any dust.*

Setting Up the Aquarium

Slate

Limestone

Pebbles

Slate
pebbles

Sandstone
chunks

Artificial
lava rock

Above: *These weathered slate rocks give an attractive and natural feel to the aquarium.*

give a more natural look. The use of rocks can give a tank a more realistic and three-dimensional feel. A slice of slate could be leaned on the side of the tank. Scattered slate pebbles can create the look of a weathered rock face. Before you place any rocks or pebbles into your tank you should assess them for how inert they are. If a rock fizzes when you drip vinegar onto it, it shows that it is calcareous (chalky). This means that it is relatively alkaline and has a high pH. Adding rocks like this may affect the pH value of your tank water. You should adhere larger rocks with silicone to the tank glass to prevent any damaging rock falls. You should not collect any pebbles or boulders from the wild as they may be contaminated. Rocks bought from an aquarium supplier must be thoroughly washed.

Both organic and artificial decorations have advantages and disadvantages. Fake decorations are long lasting, easy to clean, and are not taken from the natural environment. They won't affect the tank chemistry and you will also have more colors and sizes to choose from. On the other hand, poor quality fake decorations can look artificial and unpleasant, and may be more expensive than the real thing.

Organic decorations can look beautiful and growing plants can increase the oxygen content of the tank, but they will need replacing from time

Mopani wood

Above: *Position larger rocks and driftwood at the back of the tank.*

Stocking the Aquarium

Above: *Real plants will increase the oxygen content of the water while looking beautiful.*

to time. They may also affect the pH value of the water and driftwood may release tannin. If natural decorations are allowed to rot, this can release toxins into the tank water and you should remove them before this starts. Many fish keepers decide to use a mix of natural and manufactured decorations in their aquarium set up and this can be a great esthetic success.

Whichever decorations you decide to use, you should make sure that you clean them thoroughly before adding them to your aquarium. Don't allow anything to touch or interfere with your filter or heating equipment.

Another thing you might want to consider is using a decorative plastic background for your tank. These come in various sizes and different colors and designs. These can be plain (maybe aqua blue or black), consist of an underwater scene, fantastic landscape, sunken city or a realistic three-dimensional photograph. A background will also help to conceal your tank equipment, cables or pipe work. A background is also an inexpensive way to update an existing aquarium. Backgrounds are sold on a roll and can be trimmed to size. They should then be stretched tightly across the back of the tank and secured with adhesive tape. You can also theme your tank decorations to match your tank background. Solid textured panels or even cork tiles can also be used at the back of the tank. If they are to be fixed inside the tank, they should be placed there from the beginning.

One of the most important things to remember is that you should chose decorations that are in proportion to the size of your tank. You should also be quite sparing with them, so that your fish have plenty of room to swim around.

When you equip your tank, you need to do so in a responsible way. To do this, you should only buy natural materials from a reputable aquarium store and never collect things from the wild. Whatever you put into your tank should be thoroughly washed, without using detergents. You should double check that whatever decorations you include are suitable for your fish, and don't have any sharp edges that may hurt them. This is especially critical if you plan to keep goldfish that have fancy fins, goggle eyes or large head wens.

Finally, none of the tank decorations should touch or interfere with the heater or filtering equipment.

Above: *Backgrounds are a cheap way to update your aquarium and are sold on a roll that can be trimmed to size.*

Above: *Enthusiasts may decide to produce their own backgrounds which can be taped to the back of the aquarium.*

Aquarium Plants

A correctly heated goldfish tank will provide an ideal environment for many aquarium plants. You need to ensure that the plants you buy are healthy with strong root systems. Even so, they will need weekly feeding with aquarium plant food. You should plant larger plants toward the back and sides of your tank to create a framework for your display. Smaller plants at the front of the tank will give cover for your fish. It is often most effective to group a limited number of species in larger groupings for a stunning display of greenery.

A wide variety of plants are suitable for a heated goldfish tank. These include:

Spadeleaf Plant (*Gymnocoronis spilanthoides*)
The spadeleaf is a fast-growing stem plant with numerous white florets. Its stems are pale green. It has a very strong rate of growth.

Elodea (*Egeria densa*)

Also known as pondweed, this coldwater plant prefers hard water without the addition of carbon dioxide. It makes a very interesting plant for goldfish tanks and will be happy in water up to around 75°F (24°C).

Above: *Straight Vallis*

Left: *Spadeleaf Plant*

Straight Vallis (*Vallisneria Spiralis*)

Contrary to its scientific name, this Vallis actually has straight leaves with minimal or no twisting. It makes a nice background plant and is very easy and fast growing. Like all Vallisnerias, it's easy to grow and a good plant for beginners.

Above: *Elodea*

Aquarium Plants

Above: *Broadleaf Ludwigia*

Broadleaf Ludwigia (*Ludwigia palustris*)
This is a classic aquarium plant. The plant is a deep olive green, but under sufficient light, reddish shoots will develop near the light source.
    To plant ludwigia and achieve a stunning display of greenery in your aquarium:

1. Slide the plants out of the plant pot and separate them.

2. Make a hole in the substrate with your fingertips and hold it open.

3. Put one of the ludwigia plants into the hole and cover the roots with substrate. Press the substrate gently around the plant.

4. Plant the ludwigia plants around 1–2 inches (2.5–5 cm) apart, so that the leaves of each plant just touch.

5. If you place a few pebbles around the base of each plant, this will discourage your goldfish from digging up the plants.

Crispus (*Potamogeton crispus*)
This aquatic plant is native to North America. It prefers a medium light level and is easy to grow. It has a medium growth rate and is best planted in the mid-ground of your aquarium.

Green Milfoil (*Myriophyllum hippuroides*)
The green water milfoil is an ideal aquarium plant. It requires good light, but is not particularly fussy about the composition of the tank water and can

withstand substantial fluctuations in temperature. The delicately cut green or red foliage of the plant is surprisingly hardy. It is an excellent plant for filling in gaps in the aquascape as it will adapt to many conditions. Aquarium gravel is a perfectly acceptable substrate for this plant. Be sure to plant the stems separately to allow them to root.

The only problem that is encountered with this beauty is its tendency to trap debris. This can be easily solved by occasional gentle shakes to free any collected debris. Alternatively, place the plant near the suction or current of a filter. As with most plants, occasional fertilization would be beneficial.

Above: *Green milfoil*

Left: *Crispus*

Aquarium Plants

with umbrella-like leaves that is suitable to grow submerged. If it is illuminated brightly, numerous lidlike leaves are produced in several layers. Do not keep the plant in aquariums with voracious fish as the shoots of the plant do not root very deeply in the substrate.

Dwarf Hairgrass (*Eleocharis parvula*)
Dwarf hairgrass is a small aquatic grass plant that is used for foreground carpeting. You should cut it back prior to planting and separate each pot into six or seven pieces. You can use fine-pointed forceps to stick each plantlet into a fine-grained

Left: *Red Milfoil*

Below: *Whorled Umbrella Plant*

Red Milfoil (*Myriophyllum tuberculatum*)
Red water milfoil is the red-leaved version of green water milfoil. It can be used in the background, or mid-ground of the aquarium. The plant requires a high degree of lighting, but is fast-growing.

Whorled Umbrella Plant (*Hydrocotyle verticillata*)
The whorled umbrella plant is a lovely foreground aquarium plant and is the only plant species

Right: *Dwarf hairgrass*

substrate. One pot will cover an area of about 1½ square inches (10 sq. cm) and will rapidly grow into groundcover.

Creeping Jenny (*Lysimachia nummularia*)
Creeping Jenny is one of the most popular and best-known aquarium plants. Aquarium specimens are used to slightly higher temperatures, but should not be kept above 73°F (23°C) for long periods of time.

Above: *Creeping Jenny*

Aquarium Plants

Above: *Spatterdock*

Spatterdock (*Nuphar japonica*)
Spatterdock is an easy to grow, light green pond lily. The plant grows from a rhizome and can grow to a large size. The slightly transparent leaves of the plant create an impression of freshness and coolness. You should pinch out the longer leaves to keep the plant low and compact. Spatterdock is not suitable for a small aquarium.

Giant Sagittaria (*Sagittaria platyphylla*)
Despite its common name, giant sagittaria is actually a low-growing foreground plant. "Giant" refers to the leaf thickness, which is up to about half an inch (1.5 cm). The plant is easy to care for but requires bright lighting and a good supply of iron, either in the water or in the substrate. With time and space, the plant will produce a dense carpet of green across the aquarium floor. Successful cultivation requires a moderate temperature of between 68°F and 75°F (20°C and 24°C), intensive lighting and a nutrient-rich substrate. Good water movement seems to enhance the growth of the plant. It favors soft or medium-hard water with a weak acid pH value.

Left: *Giant Sagittaria*
Below: *Dwarf Sagittaria*

Dwarf Sagittaria (*Sagittaria pusilla*)
Sagittaria pusilla is one of the few grasslike aquarium plants that are easy to grow. They will tolerate hard water and will be happy in low to moderate light conditions. The plant does not need additional fertilizer. Nutrients in the fish food are sufficient. This aquatic plant generates very fast runners and will soon create thick grassland. It does not need cutting as it will not grow any higher than 12 inches (30 cm).

Aquarium Plants

Broad-Leaf Water Sprite/Floating Fern
(*Ceratopteris cornuta*)
Ceratopteris Cornuta is a floating aquarium plant but it can also be planted into the substrate if needed. The plant needs more light if it is planted or it will become leggy and unattractive. The plant is quite easy to maintain.

Giant Ambulia (*Limnophila aquatica*)
Limnophila aquatica is a great mid- or background aquarium plant. It is easy to grow and has beautiful white and purple flowers. Under strong light the leaf whorls can get very large.

Cardinal Plant (*Lobelia cardinalis*)
The cardinal plant has dark green to reddish leaves and responds to trimming back. It is great for planting in the mid-ground of the aquarium. It thrives with moderate lighting and fertilizer.

Right: *Broad-Leaf Water Sprite*

Opposite above: *Giant Ambulia*

Opposite below: *Cardinal Plant*

Aquarium Plants

Above: *Hornwort*

Left: *Pennywort*

Above: *Fanwort*

Pennywort (*Flexible Hydrocotyle*)
Pennywort is an attractive plant whose stems sway with the water current. It has round or kidney-shaped leaves.

Hornwort (*Ceratophyllum demersum*)
Hornwort is a free-floating or loosely anchored rootless aquarium plant. If it is pressed into substrate, Hornwort will produce modified leaves (rhizoids) that have a rootlike appearance and will keep it anchored. It can either be left floating at the aquarium surface or buried in substrate. Hornwort's stiff leaves provide cover and shelter for small fish. In addition to its water oxygenating

qualities, Hornwort is known to produce chemicals that inhibit algae growth. It is generally safe with herbivorous fish as most species don't find it very appetizing. Due to the rapid growth of the plant, it will require constant pruning to keep it in check. Cut off any excess growth with a pair of scissors.

Fanwort (*Cabomba*)
Fanwort is an aquatic plant. It has divided submerged leaves in the shape of a fan and is a great ornamental and oxygenating plant for fish tanks. The leaf whorls create attractive patterns under the tank lights.

Artificial Plants

Right: *Plastic plants are a cheaper solution to decorating your aquarium since they do not require substrate and last forever.*

Below: *A quarantine tank would benefit from the use of artificial weeds that can be scrubbed clean.*

Live plants look great but need a certain amount of maintenance. They are also prone to be eaten by your goldfish. Artificial plants last forever and can provide your fish with shelter and somewhere to spawn. They will also be colonized by the same beneficial bacteria and algae as real plants. The only thing artificial plants can't do is take nitrites out of the water. This means that you will have to pay more attention to the quality of your aquarium water. Most artificial plants are made from silk or plastic. Not being live, artificial plants don't need specialized lighting, fertilizers, nutritious substrates or carbon dioxide. Some artificial plants are weighted and don't need a substrate, making them perfect for quarantine tanks.

*Most artificial
plants are made
from silk or plastic.*

Silk Milfoil weed

Artificial plants aren't fussy about water quality and
don't affect the water conditions. They're also easy
to clean. A simple wipe with an algae pad or brush,
or a spray with the shower head will remove any
algae and detritus.

125

Filters

External Filters

External filters are very efficient, as they are filled with a large volume of filtration medium and can deal with the waste that your fish produce. External filters have powerful pumps that draw the water from the aquarium, pass it through various filtration mediums and return it to the aquarium when it has been purified. As the name suggests, external filters are positioned outside the aquarium and save space in the tank. Their positioning also means that they are easy to access for cleaning and maintenance. They are probably most suitable for slightly larger tanks. One of their few downsides is that fish with large and delicate fins may have these damaged by the intake pipes of the filter. The other is that external filters are quite bulky and need to be stored safely while they are in use, with a free flow of air around them. If your aquarium is positioned on a stand, the filter could be positioned on the shelf below.

Position the intake pipe (far left) and the return pipe at opposite sides at the back of the tank to create a good flow of water.

External filters are filled with a variety of different media in layers. These layers may include wool, activated carbon, pelleted biomedia and coarse foam. These media will gradually acquire a colony of beneficial bacteria.

Fitting the various parts of the filter correctly will ensure that it functions correctly and efficiently. The intake pipe and return pipe should be fitted at both ends of the tank to create a good flow of cleaned water. The return jet should be fitted just above or below the water surface. The intake

External filters are easy to access for maintenance.

A spraybar

Filtering media in layers ▷

An external filter saves space inside the aquarium, being sited on a shelf underneath the tank. It will deal with a large quantity of waste generated by the goldfish.

Filter wool sandwiches activated carbon.

Carbon can be kept in a bag.

Use only branded aquarium filter wool.

Pelleted biomedia support good bacteria.

A coarse foam pad traps large debris.

pipe should be passed through the aperture at the rear corner of the tank. You can cut the inlet and return pipes to a suitable length to keep everything neat and tidy. A spraybar can also be used to return water from the power filter. This should be attached to the glass at the bank of the aquarium. A multi-directional jet can also be used to deliver aerated water back into the tank. It should be positioned so that the flow is just above or below the water surface.

Left: The activated carbon used in the external filter can be put into a bag made from a stocking and tied with a loose knot.

Filters

Internal Filters

Internal filters are becoming more popular with aquarists. They are clean and easy to maintain, often producing aeration and directional flow of water. They are neatly submersed into the tank and draw the water up through a carbon and floss pad then through the bio media, ejecting the clean water to the aquarium. Internal cartridge filters enable quick and clean maintenance merely by removing the soiled carbon/floss cartridge and algae control pad and replacing monthly, all from the top of the aquarium. There is no need even to remove the filter from the aquarium.

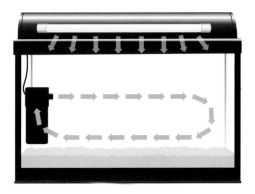

Above: *Internal tank filters circulate and oxygenate the aquarium water.*

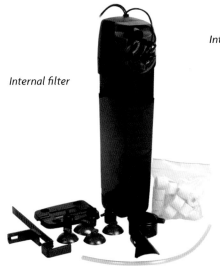

Internal filter

Internal filter

Right: *Quite a lot of tank maintenance is required with internal filters, and the gravel will require regular vacuuming.*

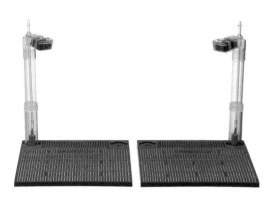

Above: *Under-gravel filters use the tank gravel as the filter medium, but don't remove fish waste.*

Under-Gravel Filters

Under-gravel filters are an option for fish bowls andsmall tanks. Effectively, they use the tank gravel as the filter medium. The devices have a base plate with holes and slits and an uplift tube that is sited under the tank substrate. Under-gravel filters draw the tank water through the holes in the plate and up into the tube. The power is supplied by either a powerhead or an airstone. The system moves the water through the gravel and oxygenates the water. The main downside of under-gravel filtration is that it requires quite a lot of tank maintenance. The gravel will require regular vacuuming, but you mustavoid sucking up the gravel itself as this will disturb the microbial balance of your tank.

Heating

Heating an Aquarium

Although goldfish don't need the same degree of warmth as tropical fish, installing a heater will ensure that your goldfish have a stable temperature that doesn't fluctuate. This is very important for the health and well-being of your fish and your aquarium plants. Although your household heating will keep the water pleasantly warm during the day, if the heating is turned off or down at night, the water may become too cold for your fish. The optimum tank temperature for goldfish is around 64°F (18°C). Slim bodied goldfish like the water a little cooler, whereas fancy goldfish need warmer water. Most water heaters vary between 25 and 300 watts in power. A 100-watt heating unit should be enough for a 24-inch (60 cm) tank. Generally

Above: *When you are buying a heater, remember as a guide that it takes about 4 watts of electricity to heat 1 gallon (4 l) of water.*

speaking, it takes about 4 watts of electricity to heat 1 gallon (4 l) of water. Combined heater/thermostats are housed in the tank. They should be positioned at an angle so that the rising heat does not pass directly over the thermostat and you should leave a gap between the heater and the substrate. The heater should never be turned on until the tank is filled and the water reaches the level specified on the unit. Heaters are usually mounted on the back wall of the tank and can be hidden behind plants, driftwood or ornaments.

It is very important that your fish can't get trapped between the heater and the glass for

Above: *Leave a gap between the bottom of the substrate and the heater.*

obvious reasons. Heater guards can be bought for most models. You should also make certain that the heater is never switched on unless the tank is filled and the water level reaches the minimum depth specified. Before your turn on the electricity make sure that any parts of the heater that need to be kept dry are free from water and leave the equipment in the water for quarter of an hour to acclimatize it to the water temperature. Make sure that your hands are also completely dry before you switch it on. When you need to remove the heater for cleaning, turn it off and leave it to cool down for a few minutes before taking it out of the water.

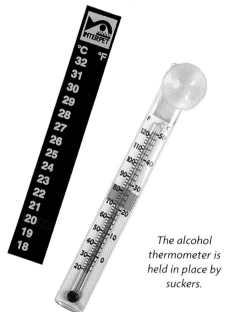

The alcohol thermometer is held in place by suckers.

You will need an aquarium thermometer to get an accurate reading of the water temperature in your aquarium and make sure that this remains constant. Some of these are fixed to the outside of the tank glass, while in-tank thermometers are stuck to the inside of the glass with rubber suckers. You should position an in-tank thermometer at the top front corner of the tank, being careful to avoid the current of your water filter. These may be either digital or conventional alcohol-filled thermometers.

Depending on the ambient temperature in your home, you will need to buy a more or less powerful tank water heater. It may be more practical to buy two smaller heaters in case one fails. These heaters are not expensive to run as they only cut in if the water temperature falls below the desired temperature. Water is 24 times more efficient at retaining heat than air, so you may find that your heater doesn't come on all that often.

If one of your fish is sick, you may find that keeping the tank slightly warmer, at around 78°F (25°C) will help them to recover more quickly and make their medication work more efficiently. The goldfish immune systems work best at this slightly higher temperature.

You should also remember that you may need to cool the water during the heat of the summer months. You can do this by placing a small table fan so that it blows across the top of the water. You can also buy cooling fans that are specifically built for this purpose. Of course, you need to be absolutely sure that the fan could not fall into or be knocked into the aquarium water.

Aquarium Lighting

The quality of aquatic life in your aquarium can be directly related to the quality of light. When designing your aquarium lighting system, your goal should be to duplicate the goldfish's natural conditions. Thanks to recent advancements in lighting technology, this has become an easier task. Adding a lighting system to your tank will enable you to view your fish and will allow your plants to flourish. The most popular lighting system for freshwater tanks used to be fluorescent tubes. They are very inexpensive, efficient, don't use much power, and run cool. This means that they won't heat up the water in your tank. A fluorescent lighting system for a fish-only tank (with artificial plants, decorative wood and ceramic decorations) should consume between 1 and 2 watts of electricity per gallon. This should be sufficient to simulate a day-night cycle. However, if you decide to use real plants in your aquarium, you will need a more efficient fluorescent lighting system that consumes between 2 and 5 watts per gallon of tank water.

LED Aquarium Lights

LED lighting is the modern choice for many aquarium keepers and is the most up-to-date form of aquarium lighting. This form of lighting uses light-emitted diodes (LEDs) as the source of illumination rather than the traditional filament in incandescent light bulbs or the gas used in fluorescent lamps. LED lights can be bought as either light strips or light tiles. Both of these options are slim and take up less room than conventional lighting.

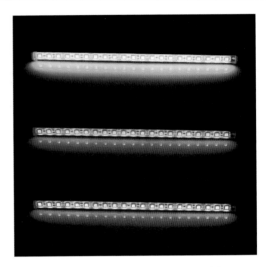

Above: *LED light tubes come in a range of intense colors.*

LED lighting is particularly useful in aquariums as it generates light without giving off a lot of heat. This results in greater efficiency and lower electrical costs. These lights are also more resistant to shock, vibration and wear. LED bulbs last for around 50,000 hours, which means that they outlast traditional bulbs by around five times.

LED aquarium lights are less expensive to run than traditional aquarium lights because they consume around 50 percent less electricity. Although LED bulbs are more expensive to buy in the first place, this means that they save money in the long run. The fact that LED bulbs don't give off much heat also means that you don't need to cool the aquarium water in the summer.

LED lighting is very efficient and so only a small number of lighting units are required to light even a large tank. This is one of the reasons that LED lights are beneficial to the environment. They generate a smaller carbon footprint, don't contain mercury and produce less physical waste (as LED systems use fewer light bulbs).

LED lights can be used in both freshwater and planted goldfish tanks. Their wide-angle beam means that they can be placed close to the water surface. This gives optimum light penetration and even light distribution. LED lights are also dimmable and programmable so that you can produce all kinds of different lighting effects in your aquarium, including sunrise, sunset, moonlight and standard daylight. This creates a more natural environment

Above: *LED spotlights can be used to light smaller aquariums.*

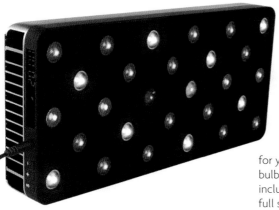

Left: *An LED light board is programmable and versatile.*

for your fish and reduces their stress levels. LED bulbs can now be bought in several different colors including white, blue, magenta, "daylight" and full spectrum light for planted aquaria. This can be adjusted to accommodate different species of plants.

Aquarium Water

Of course, the most important component of your goldfish aquarium is the water. It is very important to get the aqua environment right from the beginning so that your fish can have the best chance of a happy and healthy life. Goldfish are quite adaptable to water chemistry and will tolerate a wide range of water acidity and hardness. But you will still need to treat and condition your tap water before adding it to the tank.

Although goldfish will generally be perfectly happy with tap water, fish can't survive in water that contains chlorine. As all tap water is chlorinated, you will need to treat it before adding it to your tank. Pet stores sell testing kits that will help you to assess the level of chlorine in your water. You

Above: *Chlorinated tap water can be treated with chemicals from the pet store, such as Tapsafe.*

can de-chlorinate your water in a couple of different ways, either by treating it with chemicals from the pet store, such as Tapsafe. Alternatively, you can let your water sit for four to eight days, or longer, depending on the level of chlorine in your water and the surface area of the container the water is in. The larger the surface area of the water, the quicker the chlorine will evaporate. A clean, uncovered bucket is ideal. Make sure that your container has not had any cleaning products in it. The buckets you use for your fish tank should only be used for fish tank water and nothing else. It may also be helpful to use a bubbling airstone.

However, this process will not deal with chloramines. This substance is chlorine with added ammonia that is used to remove harmful bacteria from the domestic water supply. This can be removed with a specialist fish tank filter or specialized de-chlorinator. Both are readily available from aquarium suppliers.

Above: *Pet stores sell testing kits that will help you to assess the level of chlorine in your water.*

You should not use rainwater or purified water in your tank. Rainwater may contain pollutants, while purified water does not contain any minerals.

But before you add any fish, you should go through a process of tank cycling. Tank cycling is the method of allowing the tank to establish a natural bio-filter, which uses the tank gravel to turn highly toxic fish waste into much less harmful substances. Friendly bacteria breaks down ammonia into nitrites and then into nitrates. The process of creating this natural phenomenon can take up to two months before it achieves its peak efficiency. It is very important for the health of your fish that you don't hurry this process. Stocking your tank with too many fish before tank cycling has been established will lead to a build up of toxic substances in the tank water. This build up of poison in the water is the leading cause of fish death. During the cycling period, you shouldn't change the water, but once this is well established, you should institute regular weekly water changes.

There are several ways you can help "seed" your tank and get the water cycling process going:

1. Put in some gravel from an already established healthy tank is helpful. Be discriminating. Don't use gravel from a pet store tank, and make sure that you are absolutely certain that the tank from which you are taking the gravel is completely free from parasites and disease.

2. Adding live plants can also be helpful.

3. Use a filter system that has already been running in an established healthy tank.

4. Ask your pet store to recommend specialized products that can help the cycling process get started.

When you are ready to add the water to your tank (and the substrate is already in position) place a plate or saucer on the substrate and pour the water onto it using a clean plastic jug. This will prevent the substrate being disturbed. Continue pouring in the water until the tank is about half full. This is the stage where you can add plants and aquarium décor if this is part of your plan. An internal power filter should be installed last of all. Check for ammonia and nitrite levels at least weekly.

Above: *Start filling the tank by pouring water gently onto a plate to avoid disturbing the gravel.*

Maintenance

Left: *When the tank is maturing you can add a proprietorial brand of bacterial culture to "seed" the filter.*

Water Testing

Before you add fish to your tank, you should check the water quality very carefully for ammonia, nitrites, nitrates and the pH level. Test kits for all of these substances are simple to use and easy to buy. The most cause of problems in the early stages of setting up an aquarium is being too quick to add the fish. This is called "new tank syndrome" but it is simply ammonia or nitrite poisoning. High concentrates of these substances in the aquarium water thicken the lamellae in the fish's gills and reduce their surface area. This undermines the fishes' ability to breathe and ultimately can be fatal. This syndrome can be avoided by regular water changes and water testing. Once the fish are living in the tank, you should do this on a regular, scheduled basis. It's a good idea to keep a written record of this. Every time you are considering adding a fish, you should test the water quality again to ensure that the tank water will support another fish. If you detect a problem, do a partial water change to dilute the contaminated water in the tank.

Aquarium Maintenance

Regular aquarium maintenance is very important to maintain your aquarium as a healthy working ecosystem. This will keep your fish in good shape and your tank looking good. The best strategy is to establish a daily and weekly cleaning regime. A complete and thorough clean will be needed once each year. Your daily tank maintenance routine should include the removal of any uneaten food, a quick check on the water temperature, and a check that all your tank equipment (filters, lights, air pump and heater) are all working properly. You should also check each fish to make sure that they are in good health and showing no signs of illness or parasites.

It is very helpful to keep a written record of when you carry out this maintenance routine, and any observations of changes in the behavior of your fish.

If your aquarium water gets dirty (with a high concentrate of nitrate and phosphate) this will encourage algae to grow. Very high levels of these pollutants can even kill your fish. Algae can be removed from your tank glass with an abrasive pad, algae magnet or special algae scrapers. These come with either plastic or metal blades. Algae magnets are popular algae wipers because they are convenient and easy to use. One side of the magnet is coated with an abrasive pad and goes inside the aquarium, while the other half is coated in a soft pad for polishing the aquarium glass. Pull the magnet across the glass and it will remove algae. Floating algae magnets are the ultimate in convenience because if the inner magnet falls off, it will float to the top of the water.

The best strategy is to keep the water clean, which will discourage the growth of algae. Filtration is imperative, but water changing is fundamental to good quality tank water. But sudden changes to the water chemistry can be just as upsetting to your fish as dirty water, so you should aim to change around 10 to 20 percent of the aquarium water each week. This will dilute the pollutants in the water, while not stripping good bacteria from your aquarium. Water changing will also prevent the potentially disastrous phenomenon of pH collapse. This is when the tank water suddenly becomes very acidic. The pH can then drop from 6 or 7 to 3 or 4 overnight, with dire consequences for your fish. Regular water changes will help to maintain a good pH level in your tank. Don't use water straight from the tap in the water changes. Fill a bucket with water and leave it overnight to reach room temperature. You should also add a water conditioning de-chlorinator to remove any chlorine.

Fish eat plants and other foods containing nitrogen and excrete nitrogenous waste.

Plants use ammonia and nitrates as food and incorporate nitrogen into proteins that are eaten by fish.

Ammonia is the main waste product and is excreted from the gills and in the urine.

Bacteria living in the filter and the substrate convert toxic ammonia to nitrate, which is still poisonous to fish.

Different bacteria feed on nitrite and produce nitrate, a much less harmful substance.

Above: *Nitrogen cycle*

Maintenance

Left: *Vacuum the gravel gently to remove debris.*

Below: *Work from the top down when using an algae magnet to clean aquarium glass.*

One of the most effective ways to change the water is to use a siphon tube. Choose a self-starting siphon device to drain water from the tank into a bucket. Water changing is a good opportunity to test your aquarium water for ammonia, nitrite and the pH level. Testing the water for nitrite levels involves adding a tablet to a small sample of your tank water. This will then turn pink. The intensity of the color can be compared to a printed chart that will indicate your pH level. You should also take this opportunity to clean the tank glass, feed your aquarium plants, clean the tank cover and vacuum the tank gravel.

Vacuuming the tank gravel will remove the dirt and debris from the gravel floor of the tank. Goldfish generate a lot of solid waste that will go into solution in the tank water if it is allowed to build up on the aquarium floor. To do this properly, buy a gravel vacuum and siphon tube combined. One that self-starts will prevent you from having to suck the pipe. You should be very careful to avoid sucking up small fish or damaging your plants. The gravel vacuum will lift the gravel and spin it around inside, removing any debris. Repeat the process over the entire surface area of the tank gravel. As well as cleaning the tank floor, vacuuming will control fish parasites like whitespot. (Whitespot has a life stage that lives in the tank gravel.)

Monthly filter maintenance and cleaning is also imperative. This will keep the filter working properly, as becoming clogged can cause it to break down. Keeping the filter media (such as the sponge and filter wool) and impeller as clean as possible so that the water flow will remain constant.

Cleaning an External Filter

Turn the coupling taps to the off position and undo the plastic fasteners. Place the filter in a shallow bowl, draining away most of the water. Remove the filter motor from the canister and clean the impellor. Lift out the filter basket and remove the filter media from it. Wash the permanent media, throw away and replace the dirty filter floss and replace the exhausted activated carbon. (Carbon soaks up pollutants to the point of saturation and

Cleaning an Internal Filter

Before you start to clean the filter, make sure that it is unplugged from the electrical outlet. Lift the filter into a bowl to which you have added 1–2 inches (2.5–5 cm) of water from your tank. You can do this by siphoning, or with a jug.

Remove the impeller and its shaft and clean off the slime with a clean soft cloth. Then remove your filter media. As this also acts as a biological filter, you should never replace more than half of this at any one time. Wash it in old tank water to keep the bacteria levels high.

1. *Unplug and remove the filter, placing it into a bowl containing some tank water.*

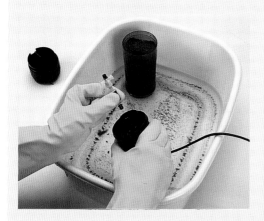

2. *Remove the impeller and shaft and clean off the slime.*

3. *Remove and rinse the sponge in the tank water so you don't remove the bacteria.*

Maintenance

then ceases to work. It should be replaced at least every four weeks.)

Nitrate and phosphate removers are also forms of chemical filtering media and also need regular replacement.

The monthly clean should also include a check of your other aquarium equipment. Service your air pump, the powerhead motor, replace any failed lighting tubes, replace the airstones and make sure that the airline is clean and unblocked. You should be particularly careful when cleaning your plastic condensation tray. These scratch easily so you should just use a clean damp cloth to wipe them. Replace the tray when they become opaque as this reduces the amount of light coming into the aquarium.

You should also clean any aquarium decorations on at least a monthly basis. This should include the aquarium rocks, driftwood, plastic plants and any other items in the tank.

Cleaning an External Filter

1. *Turn the coupling taps off and undo the nuts securing the taps. Place the filter in a shallow bowl and pour off most of the water.*

4. *Remove the filter media from the basket. Discard the soiled filter floss and the exhausted activated carbon. Both need replacing.*

2. *Remove the motor from the canister by releasing the locking tabs. Remove the impeller and clean all plastic parts with a cloth.*

3. *Remove the internal basket containing the filter media. (This filter has a one-piece assembly, but some filters have separate modules.)*

5. *Gently wash the permanent media. Loose-fill the special bag with fresh carbon and reassemble. Replace the motor unit. Couple the filter to the taps.*

6. *The plastic condensation tray should be cleaned with a clean, damp cloth to avoid scratching it.*

CARING FOR YOUR GOLDFISH

Feeding Your Goldfish

Your goldfish are completely dependent on you to look after them properly and to give them a happy life. You must feed them the right amount of the right food, and this is crucial to their good health and happiness. Variety is very important, and you should aim to mimic the kind of food that your fish would eat in the wild. Goldfish also enjoy the occasional treat, as well as their basic food.

It is very important to feed the correct amount of food to your fish. Excessive food will pollute the water, clog your filtration system and ultimately poison your fish. A good rule of thumb is that your fish shouldn't feed for more than five to six minutes a day in total. It is best to divide this feeding time into two or three regular feeding sessions of one to two minutes each. Goldfish do not have stomachs, so their digestive system can't handle too much food at once; it's much kinder to feed them little and often, keeping the five to six minute rule in mind. Although this doesn't sound like much, remember that goldfish are cold blooded and require less food than warm-blooded creatures (like mammals) as they don't need to absorb calories to maintain body heat. Healthy goldfish are usually enthusiastic eaters and will feed greedily until they are satisfied. You should stop as soon as they start to lose interest, or you notice a slight bulge in their tummies.

Your goldfish will soon come to associate your

Above: *It is a helpful rule to use that your goldfish shouldn't feed for more than five to six minutes a day.*

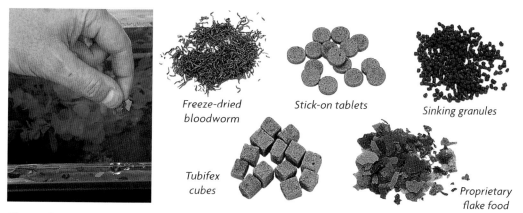

Freeze-dried bloodworm

Stick-on tablets

Sinking granules

Tubifex cubes

Proprietary flake food

Above: *There are several kinds of dry goldfish food available. Flakes float and pellets sink.*

appearance with feeding time, and may start to wag their fins and beg for your attention when you pass by the tank. Although this is charming, you should resist the urge to feed them more often.

When you choose your feeding regime, it's worth remembering that goldfish are omnivores. But although their diet can include meat, they should also be fed a good diet that includes lots of greens. In the tank environment, they will also eat microscopic plants and animals, aquatic plants, insects and crustaceans.

It's essential that your goldfish have a varied diet. Variety means that your goldfish will receive the right amount of nutrients for health and strong growth. You should try to include three main food types in your goldfish's diet: dry food, live (or freeze-dried) food and a selection of vegetables.

You can use one or two dry goldfish food brands

as a stable diet daily. It's better not to use the same brand all the time, as none of these contain everything that your goldfish needs. Mix in live or freeze-dried food several times a week and offer your fish vegetables and/or fruit once or twice a week. This mixed diet will keep your goldfish interested in their food and should keep them active, happy, and healthy.

Different types of dry goldfish food are widely available. Flakes are designed to float on the tank water, while pellets are designed to sink to the bottom of the tank. Both are suitable for goldfish as they are both top- and

Caring for Your Goldfish

bottom-feeders. They thoroughly enjoyed sifting through the substrate to see if any tasty tidbits are lurking there. You should ensure that whatever food you feed is small enough for your smallest fish to enjoy. Flakes and pellets both have advantages and disadvantages. Floating food can encourage your fish to suck in air, which can lead to buoyancy and swim bladder problems. This is especially true of some fancy goldfish. On the other hand, any excess floating flakes can be quickly and easily removed from the tank, while excess pellets can get stuck under rocks and pollute the tank water.

If you plan to keep short-bodied and/or egg-shaped fancy goldfish varieties, it is a good idea to soak dry food briefly before feeding it to them. Dry food expands as it absorbs water, and if your fancy goldfish eats a pellet before it expands, it may clog its intestines. As these breeds are also prone to swim bladder and buoyancy problems, surface feeding can be problematic (as they will gulp in air with the food) and soaking it will ensure that it sinks below the surface. To make goldfish food easier to digest, simply fill a cup with aquarium water and soak the dry food for 5 to 10 seconds

▶ *Live Food*

Live food such as glassworms, daphnia, brine shrimp, tubifex worms and aquarium snails are a great source of protein for your goldfish. Use it to bring them to show condition, for young fish and especially if you are thinking of breeding them. Buy it in small quantities as you need it.

Daphnia

Above: *Aquarium snails*

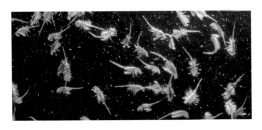

Above: *Brine shrimp*

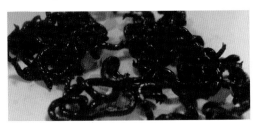

Above: *Tubifex worms*

Above: *Goldfish enjoy eating aquatic plants such as duckweed as part of their diet.*

before feeding it to the fish. Soaking the food for longer than this can be detrimental as water-soluble vitamins like vitamin C may get leached out. Green vegetables and fresh fruit will also benefit your fish's digestion.

Goldfish also enjoy live food, which is an excellent source of protein. Some fish keepers feed their fish with live food to get them in condition for breeding and it is also good for young fish. Fancy goldfish with head wens seem to benefit greatly from live food being included in their diet. Live foods include brine shrimp, daphnia, tubifex worms, glassworms, and aquarium snails. The latter are a particular goldfish delicacy. Goldfish also enjoy eating live aquatic plants, including duckweed. However, there is a small chance that live food can carry bacteria that could make your fish ill. You should buy it in small quantities and store it carefully, according to the instructions. Frozen or freeze-dried foods are less risky, and your fish will receive all of the nutrients of live food without the risk of infection. Brine shrimp, bloodworms, tubifex worms, krill, plankton, Mysis

Above: *Fancy goldfish with head wens seem to benefit greatly from live food being included in their feeding regime.*

Above: *Tubifex cubes will stick to the side of the tank where the fish can nibble at them.*

Right: *For convenience you can buy dried shrimp food.*

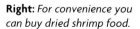

Caring for Your Goldfish

shrimp, cyclops, daphnia and mosquito larvae are all available freeze-dried. Krill is especially effective in boosting your fishes' carotene levels, which will help red pigmentation and promotes beautiful contrasting colors. Although they are from marine environments, squid and algae are also popular with goldfish and are excellent sources of nutrition. Freeze-dried food can be fed once or twice a week to supplement your goldfishes' basic diet of dry food. It should always be thoroughly thawed before being fed to your fish, and fed as soon as it is thawed.

Natural greenstuffs should also be included in the diet of your goldfish, and offered two or three times a week. These will help your fish to avoid constipation and buoyancy problems. Soft fruit and vegetables including peas (with the skins removed, halved and broken into pieces), boiled zucchini, boiled broccoli, diced boiled potatoes, orange pieces, banana pieces and lettuce leaves

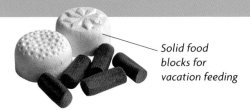

Solid food blocks for vacation feeding

are all popular with goldfish. Pet stores can also supply fresh seaweed. Any uneaten vegetable matter should be taken out of the tank as quickly as possible.

Many pet stores also sell special goldfish treats. These may include tablets and tubifex cubes that stick onto the aquarium glass. Your fish will cluster around these as the treats disintegrate. As your pet goldfish become more accustomed to you, they will even take treats and tidbits direct from your fingers!

Vacation Feeding

If you are planning to go away for a couple of days, you can buy a "vacation block." This is a compressed block of fish food that will gradually dissolve in the aquarium. You can also use timed-release goldfish feeders. These methods are only suitable for a short period of time, as it will limit the variety of your fishes' diet, and lessen their interest in their food. It would be better to have someone come in and feed your fish with their usual diet and treats. You should leave written instructions and make sure that you explain the dangers of overfeeding. Measuring out the food in advance is a good idea. The person feeding your fish should also check that your tank equipment is all working properly. It might also be a good idea to leave your vet's telephone number in case of any problems.

Zucchini, lettuce and broccoli are good greenstuffs for your goldfish.

Goldfish Health Care

Goldfish are pretty hardy creatures and don't often become sick. The most important contribution that you can make to their good health is to maintain a clean and healthy aquarium and feed your fish a varied diet. Generally speaking, experienced aquarists have healthy fish. Bad water conditions are the most common reason for a goldfish to become ill as they stress your fish and leave them prone to infection. But even when kept under the best conditions, goldfish aren't entirely immune to disease. A written record of your water tests, water changes or any changes in the behavior of your goldfish my help you to pinpoint what has caused a fish to become ill.

The most important thing is to catch any illness at an early stage. This is so that they can be treated quickly and to prevent illness infecting other fish. Some goldfish infections can prove to be fatal in a matter of days. For this reason, it can be very helpful to keep some basic fish medicines at home.

Even if their illness isn't contagious, you should put your sick goldfish in a quarantine tank. This is a smaller tank where the sick fish is separated from your other goldfish. This helps your goldfish recuperate without being stressed. It also means that your healthy fish won't receive medication that they don't need (this is called being "over-medicated").

You should watch for any change in your fishes' appearance or behavior. You should pay particular attention to any damage to your fishes' skin or fins, sudden bloating, feces trailing from the vent, spots, sores or skin discoloration. A sick fish may be more or less active than usual, may lose interest in food, float on the surface, swim sideways, lose weight or sit on the bottom of the tank. Fish with parasites may try to scratch themselves on objects in your aquarium.

Above: *Luckily goldfish are quite hardy and don't often become sick.*

COMMON FISH ILLNESSES

Cloudy Eyes

Cyst or Tumor

Dropsy

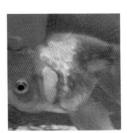

Fungal Infection

Bacterial Infection
Bacterial infections can result in a range of symptoms, including a shrunken or swollen stomach, protruding scales, protruding eyes, bloodshot skin and ulcers. A serious bacterial infection is usually related to fish being kept in stressful conditions. Small ulcers may respond to antibacterial remedies, but anything more serious than this should be shown to a vet.

Cloudy Eyes
If just one of the fish's eyes is cloudy it is likely to be the result of a physical injury. If both eyes are affected it is likely to be due to poor water conditions or diet.

If the latter, you should test your water and offer better food.

Congenital Deformities
Goldfish can suffer from various congenital deformities including missing gill covers, missing eyes, kinked spines, absent or misshapen fins. Although these deformities may not trouble your fish, don't breed from these individuals.

Cysts or Tumors
Fishes can often have cysts or tumors. These do not spread to other fish or undermine the health of the fish.

Dropsy
Protruding scales that

make the surface of the body look like a pinecone can indicate dropsy. Dropsy is often caused by bacterial infections and is sometimes incurable.

Fin Rot
If your fish exhibits ragged, pale or bloody fins, they may be suffering from fin rot. This is a bacterial infection following a period of stress, poor water quality or a physical injury. The delicate tissues between the fin rays can be eroded by the condition. Simply changing the water and separating your goldfish from more aggressive fish can solve this problem. For mild

cases of fin rot, you can use a commercial fin rot treatment. But for more severe cases, you will need to take your fish to the vet.

Fungal Infection
Whitish, fluffy patches, discolored spots or raised bumps that appear anywhere on the body or fins might indicate a fungal infection. This can be the result of a physical injury or severe stress. It can be treated with an over-the-counter fungal remedy. Quarantine the affected goldfish immediately and run some water tests on the main aquarium to determine what caused the goldfish disease symptoms.

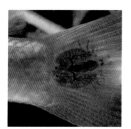

Lice

Pop Eye

Swim Bladder

Whitespot

Leech

Lice, Anchor Worms, Leeches and Flukes

These multicellular parasites will show up on fish as wormlike or round appendages, usually gray or brown in color. An affected fish may have pale gills. They are virtually impossible to treat at home and you should consult a vet immediately.

Parasitic Infection

Pale, slimy skin showing excess mucus might indicate a parasitic infection. It can also be the result of poor water conditions, but if a water test indicates that your water quality is good, treat your fish with a proprietary external parasite cure. If this doesn't seem effective, take your fish to the vet. Swift action is needed to save your fish.

Pop Eye

If one or both eyes of your goldfish are abnormally large, this could be an early symptom of pop eye or a bacterial infection.

Respiratory Infection

Rapid, heavy breathing may indicate a respiratory infection or poor water conditions. You should test the aquarium water quality and oxygen level as a matter of urgency. If these are normal, take your fish to the vet.

Swim Bladder Disorders

Fish that seem to have lost their balance, or have an abnormal tendency to float, sink or lie on one side but seem otherwise healthy may have swim bladder problems. Some fancy goldfish varieties seem more prone to this condition. The problem can be managed by maintaining excellent water quality and feeding a varied diet. If this doesn't cure the problem, consult a vet.

Whitespot

Pinhead-sized white spots on the fish's body, skin and fins usually indicate a whitespot infection. This is an infectious parasitic infection that feeds on your fishes' bodily fluids. It can be cured by a proprietary whitespot remedy. Whitespot is also known as freshwater ich or ick. The infection usually happens when your fishes' immune system is low. Left untreated, it can be fatal.

MEDICAL ADVICE

If you have concerns about your fishes' health, seek professional advice. The most important thing is to diagnose any health problems quickly and correctly so that you can use the correct remedy. Don't hesitate to ask for help to enable you to do this. Using more than one medicine could aggravate your fishes' ill health. An aquatic pet store might be able to advise you, or your vet. It's well worth investing in a small plastic carrying tank that you can use to take a sick fish to the vet. If you are treating your fish yourself, you should be extremely careful to use any medication exactly as the instructions direct. It is very important to use it in the correct concentration. You should dilute any medication in aquarium water in a clean jug. This will prevent any dangerous hot spots of the medication in the tank water. You can then add the diluted medication to

Medication should be added to some tank water and mixed in a clean jug before returning the medicated water to the tank.

the tank. Some medications can be added to the whole tank without harming the other fish, but some medications can be harmful and should be administered in an isolation or quarantine tank.

The Quarantine Tank

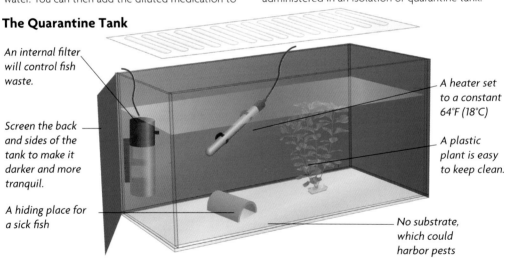

An internal filter will control fish waste.

Screen the back and sides of the tank to make it darker and more tranquil.

A hiding place for a sick fish

A heater set to a constant 64°F (18°C)

A plastic plant is easy to keep clean.

No substrate, which could harbor pests

Setting Up a Quarantine Tank

A 10–20-gallon (38–76 l) tank should be sufficient unless you have larger fish. Fill it with water from the main aquarium. Test this water for pH, ammonia, nitrite and nitrate to ensure that it is suitable for your sick fish. You will need to equip the isolation tank with some type of filtration. A filter that hangs on the back of the tank is fine for this, but just use filter floss in the filter as activate carbon will filter out any medication you add the water and defeat the purpose of the exercise. You will also need a tank heater so that you can maintain the water at a constant temperature of at least 64°F (18°C). A thermometer is important for at-a-glace temperature monitoring. It's also very important to the isolation tank water well aerated. A powerhead or airstone will increase the surface agitation. This will speed the loss of carbon dioxide at the water surface. Remember that all of this equipment should be dedicated to your quarantine tank and should not be used on your full-sized tank. Screening the back and sides of the tank and avoiding tank lighting will create a relaxing and low key environment. Light can also break down medication. You should make sure that it is comfortable and relaxing for the sick goldfish, with maybe a single plastic plant or plastic cave as a hiding place for nervous fish. A completely bare tank will stress your fish, but you should leave the bottom of your quarantine tank bare, without any substrate. Part of the life cycle of some aquatic parasites involves living in the substrate so removing this will interrupt this. In the case of larger parasites or worms, you will be able to spot them on the bare tank base.

Left: *Aeration in treatment tanks can help oxygen uptake and carbon dioxide loss at the water surface.*

When you add your sick fish to the quarantine tank make sure that you use a clean fish net – not the same one that you use for the main tank. Once your fish has been treated and recovered, it's a good idea to keep the fish in isolation for at least a week or two. Some fish keepers recommend that you should extend this to a couple of months.

You should continue to test the water in the isolation tank as long as your fish is in there. It is very important that sick fish are not further stressed by poor water quality.

You can also use your isolation tank to quarantine any new fish that you buy. You will be able to check that they are fit and well before adding them to your main tank. Two or three weeks will give you chance to observe their health and well-being. If they do develop any health issues, you can also easily medicate them in the isolation tank.

BREEDING GOLDFISH

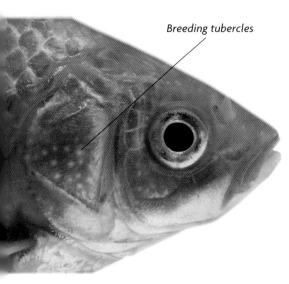

Breeding tubercles

Above: *During the breeding season male fish have breeding tubercles, little white spots, on their gill covers.*

Enlarged female vent

Breeding goldfish is not for beginner fish keepers. Breeding goldfish in an aquarium will require quite a bit of preparation and extra equipment. You will also need to establish a nursery tank. This is because in their natural habitat, goldfish have more, space, oxygen and plants to leave their eggs on. Fish eggs and hatchlings will also need extra care.

Most goldfish are ready to breed from the age of one to two years old, but usually breed best at the age of three. Goldfish spawn once a month between April and August, when the weather is warmer. Raising the water temperature in the tank to 70°F (21°C) can counterfeit this. Increasing the hours that the tank is lit will also help to create an artificial summertime.

Sexing goldfish can be quite difficult, even in the breeding season. The female usually has a more rounded appearance during this time (this is easier to observe from above). The female's swollen abdomen is due to the development of eggs in the ovaries. When she is ready to spawn, her vent becomes protruded. During the breeding season, male fish have breeding tubercles (these look like white pimples) dotted over their gill covers and pectoral fins. These markings are also known as spawning rash. (Don't confuse it with whitespot.) When he is ready to spawn, the male goldfish's vent becomes more open and longer.

During the breeding season, male fish will start to pursue female goldfish, creating quite a splash. They are attracted by the pheromones that the female goldfish releases into the water. This lets the males know that they are ready to breed. The males start to produce milt (fish sperm) at this time. The chase will continue until the male nudges the female's stomach area. This encourages her to release her eggs. The male goldfish then releases his milt and fertilizes them. During the mating season, male goldfish can sometimes appear as though they are being aggressive toward female fish, constantly nudging them and forcing them to release their eggs. If this goes on for more than a week, you should move the females into a separate tank to give them some rest. This will prevent the female goldfish from losing too many scales and getting overstressed (this will affect their immune system).

This process of external fertilization means that both the male milt (soft roe) and the female eggs (hard roe) are released from the male and female fish outside their bodies. Females can lay up to about a thousand eggs, but only a small portion of these become fertilized and grow into healthy adults.

Several factors will be helpful in helping your fish to breed successfully:

Above: *During the breeding season the male goldfish will pursue the female fish.*

1. Add protein to your fishes' diet, such as daphnia, insect larvae, bloodworms and brine shrimp. You should also add vegetables and fruit to keep them healthy and make sure that they are not constipated. Earthworms are also good conditioning food.

2. Fresh water will give your fish more energy. Change 20 percent of the tank water every day to remove the waste resulting from their extra food. Always treat the new water with purifying conditioner before adding it to the tank.

Above: *The female lays her eggs in dense aquatic vegetation.*

Breeding Goldfish

Making the Spawning Mop

You will need:
a skein of dark green nylon wool
a wine cork
a letter-sized hardback book
a pair of scissors

1. *Wind the wool around the short side of the book about 30 times. Cut off the surplus.*
2. *Thread another piece of wool about 8 inches (20 cm) of wool under the strands and secure the ends with a very tight knot.*
3. *Cut through the yarn opposite the knot to create two equal strands each side of the tie.*
4. *Turn the book over and cut the wool around the back right along the middle. This will create two equal-length strands.*
5. *Wash the mop in warm water before you use it. Rinse and dry it.*
6. *Tie or pin the cork to the top of the mop. This will enable it to float on the top of the water and resemble natural plants in the wild.*
7. *Add the mop to your breeding tank.*

Secure the strands with a knot.

Cut through the loops.

Wash the wool in warm water before you use it in the tank.

3. Maintain a consistent water temperature of 70°F (21°C) during the day and 50°F (10°C) during the night.

4. You will need to sex your male and female fish. Then separate them into different tanks for three days. This will create a greater desire to breed. You will need to prepare this second tank a week in advance to make sure that it has been properly cycled. Later, this can become the "fry tank" for the young goldfish.

5. Reintroduce the male and female fish after three days. You should put two males and one female together, in the largest possible tank. A simple sponge filter is best as this will not suck in larvae or fish fry. This controlled spawning will mean that you can choose the parents of your baby fish and to produce fry that have desirable colors and characteristics.

6. In the wild, goldfish mate among plants and vegetation. The females' eggs adhere to these and are then fertilized by the male fishes' milt. To create a natural environment in your aquarium you will need to create a spawning mop to imitate these conditions.

With luck, your fish should spawn within a few days.

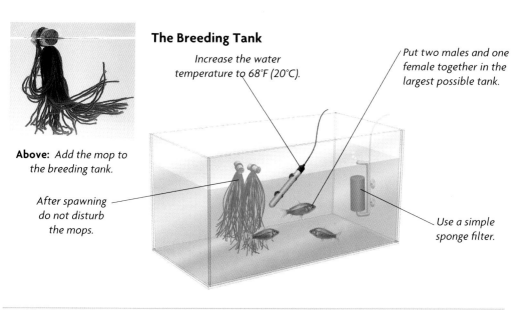

The Breeding Tank

Increase the water temperature to 68°F (20°C).

Put two males and one female together in the largest possible tank.

Above: *Add the mop to the breeding tank.*

After spawning do not disturb the mops.

Use a simple sponge filter.

Breeding Goldfish

The Fry Tank

You will need to set up a fry tank in time for your fish eggs being fertilized. This will take at least a week, so you should begin doing this before you add the spawning mop. The fry tank must be properly cycled. The secret to ensure that the cycling process starts properly is to use 20 percent of water from the main aquarium.

Steps to setting up a fry tank:
1. Use a 10-gallon (38 l) aquarium.
2. Make sure that the fry tank temperature is the same as the breeding tank.
3. Use a simple sponge filter to prevent the fry getting sucked up.
4. The fry tank should have a bare bottom with no gravel so that any dirt, debris and dead fry will be easy to see and remove.
5. Ensure the water is no deeper than 6 inches (15 cm) so the fry can get to the water surface to feed.
6. Use a water heater to keep the temperature at an even 6 inches (15 cm).

Spawning the Eggs

Remove the eggs from the spawning mop as soon as you see them, otherwise these will be eaten by the adult goldfish. Do this by rinsing the mop gently into the fry tank to release the eggs and milt. Clear eggs will hatch whereas cloudy ones will not. At an even temperature of 70°F (21°C), the eggs will hatch in about three to five days. The newly hatched fry will look like tiny hairs.

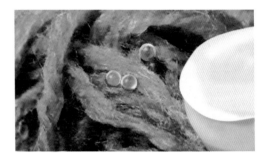

Above: *Eggs on the spawning mop*

Feeding Your Fry

The newly hatched fry are too small to eat the same food as adult goldfish. For a couple of days, they will survive by absorbing the food from their yolk sacs. When the tiny fry swim away from the spawning mop (this will be after 48 hours or so), you can start to feed them liquid fry food, which contains microscopic organisms and algae. This liquid food is especially designed for fish fry.

The protein in hard-boiled egg yolk will also help the fry to grow.

In their first month of life, you should feed the fry between three and six times a day.

At two months, the fry will be able to manage more substantial food. Newly-hatched brine shrimp make an excellent snack for them. You can also buy brine shrimp eggs from pet stores to hatch at home. Algae also make an excellent food for goldfish babies.

Infusoria are also a popular food for fry. These are single-celled organisms that can also be

should aim to do a water change every other day. You will need to be very careful not to siphon the fry out of the tank.

For the first four months, feed the fry three times a day, giving them only what they can eat in two minutes to prevent the water from becoming dirty.

So long as you don't have any large fish in your aquarium, you should be able to transfer your fry back to the main aquarium when they are around ¾ inch (2 cm) long. This can take as little as six weeks. But you should make sure that your filter will not suck them up. But your young fry will still need frequent and specialist feeding.

Above: *The fish fry will need to reach a length of ¾ inch (2 cm) before they join the main aquarium.*

Right: *These Moors are two and a half months old.*

cultivated at home. Take a piece of fruit such as banana, or a piece of lightly boiled potato and place it in a jar with some aquarium water. Put it in direct sunlight for a week. After a week in a warm spot, the water will become cloudy with infusoria. You can feed three tablespoons of the water to the fry tank at each feeding.

Regular water changes in the first month will provide optimum conditions for your fry, so you

Showing Your Goldfish

Above: *Body shape is just one of the judging criteria; color, fins and condition are also studied.*

Above: *Attending shows is a good way to meet fellow goldfish enthusiasts.*

If you have bred your own high-quality goldfish, you may wish to show them competitively. Many goldfish owners enjoy the fun and excitement of freshwater fish shows. It also gives them an opportunity to learn the current breed standards for your variety of goldfish. Seeing and comparing your fish to those of other hobbyists will greatly accelerate your goldfish breeding skills. You may well find a dedicated goldfish club in your area. Although there are a limited number of professional goldfish shows, most goldfish shows are open to amateurs and hobbyists. Some shows are for specific types of fancy goldfish.

All goldfish are judged on five different criteria; body shape, special characteristics, color, fins, and condition and deportment. Twenty points are awarded for each category, a total of a hundred points. The criteria will differ from breed to breed, but the characteristics will be set out for each goldfish type and you should be able to gain an idea of how close your fish has come to the ideal. Show prizes are usually quite modest (perhaps an aquarium, fish food or a small trophy) but a show-winning fish can increase in value as breeding stock.

You should be aware that as in all competitive activities, some people take goldfish shows very seriously. As your pets may be subjected to harsh criticism, you can't afford to be overly sensitive if you decide to show them. But if you can accept honest criticism, you will learn a lot and may be able to return with a real winner sometime in the future.

Right: *The characteristics will be set out for each goldfish type, like this fancy Pompom and you should be able to gain an idea of how close your fish has come to the ideal.*

Below: *Many owners will enjoy the fun and excitement of competing in a freshwater fish show.*